# TEACHER'S PET PUBLICATIONS

PUZZLE PACK
for
I Know Why the Caged Bird Sings

based on the book by
Maya Angelou

Written by
Mary B. Collins

© 2005 Teacher's Pet Publications
All Rights Reserved

The materials in this packet are copyrighted
by Teacher's Pet Publications, Inc.

These pages may be duplicated by the purchaser
for use in the purchaser's own classroom.

Copying any of these materials and distributing them
for any other purpose is a violation of the copyright laws.

© 2005 Teacher's Pet Publications, Inc.
www.tpet.com

INTRODUCTION
If you already own the LitPlan for this title, this Puzzle Pack will refresh your Unit Resource Materials and Vocabulary Resource Materials sections plus give you additional materials you can substitute into the tests. If you do not already have a complete LitPlan, these pages will give you some supplemental materials to use with your own plan. There are two main groups of materials: one set for unit words (such as characters' names, symbols, places, etc.) and one set for vocabulary words associated with the book.

WORD LIST
There is a word list for both the unit words and the vocabulary words. These lists show you which words are being used in the materials and the clues or definitions being used for those words. You may want to give students a word list with clues/definitions to help them, or you may want students to only have a word list (without clues/definitions) if you want them to work a little harder. Both are available for duplication. The word lists can also be your "calling key" for the bingo games.

FILL IN THE BLANK AND MATCHING
There are 4 each of the fill in the blank and matching worksheets for both the unit and vocabulary words. These pages can be used either as extra worksheets for students or as objective parts of a unit test. They can be done individually if students need extra help or as a whole class activity to review the material covered.

MAGIC SQUARES
The magic squares not only reinforce the material covered but also work on reasoning and math skills. Many teachers have told us that their students really enjoy doing these!

WORD SEARCH PUZZLES
The word search words go in all directions, as indicated on your answer keys. Two of the word search puzzles have the clues listed rather than the words. This makes the puzzle a little more difficult, but it reinforces the material better. Two word search puzzles have words only for students who find the clue puzzles too difficult.

CROSSWORD PUZZLES
Both unit and vocabulary word sections have 4 crossword puzzles.

BINGO CARDS
There are 32 individual bingo cards for the unit words and 32 individual bingo cards for the vocabulary words. You can use your word list as a "call list," calling the words at random and marking them off of your list as you go, or you could use the flash cards by cutting them apart and drawing the words at random from a hat (or box or whatever). To make a better review, you might ask for the definition and spelling of each word as you call it out–or you could call out the definitions and have students tell you the words they need to look for on the puzzle.

JUGGLE LETTERS
The vocabulary juggle letter game is intended to help students learn the spellings of the words. One sheet has the definitions listed on it as an extra help for students who need it or to reinforce the definitions if you choose to do so.

FLASH CARDS
We've included a set of vocabulary flash cards you can duplicate, cut, and fold for your students. Some teachers make a few sets for general use by the class; others make a set for each student. Some teachers duplicate them for each student and have the students cut & fold their own. You can cut out just the words and put them in a hat, have each student pick out one word and write the definition and a sentence for that word. Students then swap words and papers, with the next student adding a sentence of his own under the last one. You can have students swap as many times as you like. Each time the student will read the sentences written prior to his own and then add a sentence. You can cut out the words and definitions separately and play "I Have; Who Has?" Each student in the room draws a word and definition. The first student says, "I have (the name of the word). Who has the definition?" The student with the definition reads it then says, "I have (the name of the vocabulary word she has). Who has the definition?" The round continues until all words and definitions have been given.

Caged Bird Unit Word List

No.	Word	Clue/Definition
1.	ANGELES	Los ___; Daddy Bailey's home
2.	ANGELOU	Maya ___; author
3.	BAILEY	Marguerite's brother
4.	BLONDE	Marguerite dreamed she would one day have __ hair and blue eyes
5.	CULLLINAN	Mrs. ____ changed Marguerite's name
6.	DOLORES	Cut Marguerite in a fight
7.	DONLEAVY	His graduation speech made Marguerite angry and sick
8.	FLOWERS	Mrs. ____ gave Marguerite the gift of books
9.	FRANCISCO	San ___; Marguerite's home in high school
10.	FREEMAN	Mr. ____ sexually abused Marguerite
11.	GIGGLE	What Louise taught Marguerite to do
12.	GOD	According to Marguerite, he was white but not prejudiced
13.	GRANDMOTHER	This Baxter was precinct captain in St. Louis
14.	HENDERSON	Momma's last name
15.	HERO	The ___ is that man who is offered only crumbs but is able to make a feast
16.	JOYCE	Bailey's first love
17.	JUNKYARD	Marguerite lived here for one month
18.	KINGDOM	Marguerite described Bailey as her ___ Come
19.	KIRWIN	Teacher in love with information & treated students respectfully
20.	KLAN	Searched for a Black man
21.	LINCOLN	Dr. ___ wouldn't treat Marguerite's tooth
22.	LOUIS	St. ___; Daddy Bailey took children there
23.	LOUISE	Marguerite's first friend
24.	LOYAL	Attribute of Baxter clan
25.	MARY	Marguerite's new name
26.	MEXICO	Marguerite drove home from this place
27.	MOMMA	Owner of the store
28.	MONROE	Sister ___ got carried away at church services
29.	MRS	This title for Momma in court proved her worth and dignity
30.	PREGNANCY	Result of Marguerite's seduction
31.	PURSE	Sister Monroe hit Rev. Thomas with her ___
32.	SEGREGATION	It was complete in Stamps
33.	SHAKESPEARE	Marguerite's first white love
34.	STAMPS	City in Arkansas where author lived
35.	STREET	Marguerite was first Negro to work on the ____ cars
36.	TAYLOR	Mr. ___ saw his dead wife in a dream
37.	TRAIN	Johnson children's method of travel to Stamps
38.	TRASH	Powhite___ mocked and insulted Momma
39.	VIVIAN	Mother Dear; ___ Baxter
40.	WEALTH	Enviable attribute of whites
41.	WILLIE	Uncle ___ was crippled as a child

Caged Bird Fill In The Blank 1

_____
_____
_____
_____
_____
_____
_____
_____
_____
_____
_____
_____
_____
_____
_____
_____
_____
_____
_____
_____

1. According to Marguerite, he was white but not prejudiced
2. Mrs. ____ changed Marguerite's name
3. This Baxter was precinct captain in St. Louis
4. San ___; Marguerite's home in high school
5. Mr. ____ sexually abused Marguerite
6. Cut Marguerite in a fight
7. Powhite___ mocked and insulted Momma
8. Marguerite was first Negro to work on the ____ cars
9. His graduation speech made Marguerite angry and sick
10. Bailey's first love
11. Searched for a Black man
12. Maya ___; author
13. The ___ is that man who is offered only crumbs but is able to make a feast
14. Enviable attribute of whites
15. Mr. ___ saw his dead wife in a dream
16. Attribute of Baxter clan
17. This title for Momma in court proved her worth and dignity
18. Los ___; Daddy Bailey's home
19. Owner of the store
20. Johnson children's method of travel to Stamps

Caged Bird Fill In The Blank 1 Answer Key

GOD	1. According to Marguerite, he was white but not prejudiced
CULLLINAN	2. Mrs. ____ changed Marguerite's name
GRANDMOTHER	3. This Baxter was precinct captain in St. Louis
FRANCISCO	4. San ___; Marguerite's home in high school
FREEMAN	5. Mr. ____ sexually abused Marguerite
DOLORES	6. Cut Marguerite in a fight
TRASH	7. Powhite___ mocked and insulted Momma
STREET	8. Marguerite was first Negro to work on the ____ cars
DONLEAVY	9. His graduation speech made Marguerite angry and sick
JOYCE	10. Bailey's first love
KLAN	11. Searched for a Black man
ANGELOU	12. Maya ___; author
HERO	13. The ___ is that man who is offered only crumbs but is able to make a feast
WEALTH	14. Enviable attribute of whites
TAYLOR	15. Mr. ___ saw his dead wife in a dream
LOYAL	16. Attribute of Baxter clan
MRS	17. This title for Momma in court proved her worth and dignity
ANGELES	18. Los ___; Daddy Bailey's home
MOMMA	19. Owner of the store
TRAIN	20. Johnson children's method of travel to Stamps

Caged Bird Fill In The Blank 2

_____

1. Mr. ___ saw his dead wife in a dream
2. Marguerite lived here for one month
3. Dr. ___ wouldn't treat Marguerite's tooth
4. According to Marguerite, he was white but not prejudiced
5. Owner of the store
6. This title for Momma in court proved her worth and dignity
7. Bailey's first love
8. Marguerite drove home from this place
9. San ___; Marguerite's home in high school
10. Uncle ___ was crippled as a child
11. Enviable attribute of whites
12. Marguerite was first Negro to work on the _____ cars
13. Marguerite described Bailey as her ___ Come
14. His graduation speech made Marguerite angry and sick
15. Marguerite dreamed she would one day have __ hair and blue eyes
16. Sister Monroe hit Rev. Thomas with her ___
17. Marguerite's first friend
18. City in Arkansas where author lived
19. Los ___; Daddy Bailey's home
20. Johnson children's method of travel to Stamps

Caged Bird Fill In The Blank 2 Answer Key

TAYLOR	1. Mr. ___ saw his dead wife in a dream
JUNKYARD	2. Marguerite lived here for one month
LINCOLN	3. Dr. ___ wouldn't treat Marguerite's tooth
GOD	4. According to Marguerite, he was white but not prejudiced
MOMMA	5. Owner of the store
MRS	6. This title for Momma in court proved her worth and dignity
JOYCE	7. Bailey's first love
MEXICO	8. Marguerite drove home from this place
FRANCISCO	9. San ___; Marguerite's home in high school
WILLIE	10. Uncle ___ was crippled as a child
WEALTH	11. Enviable attribute of whites
STREET	12. Marguerite was first Negro to work on the ____ cars
KINGDOM	13. Marguerite described Bailey as her ___ Come
DONLEAVY	14. His graduation speech made Marguerite angry and sick
BLONDE	15. Marguerite dreamed she would one day have __ hair and blue eyes
PURSE	16. Sister Monroe hit Rev. Thomas with her ___
LOUISE	17. Marguerite's first friend
STAMPS	18. City in Arkansas where author lived
ANGELES	19. Los ___; Daddy Bailey's home
TRAIN	20. Johnson children's method of travel to Stamps

Caged Bird Fill In The Blank 3

1. The ___ is that man who is offered only crumbs but is able to make a feast
2. Marguerite's first white love
3. Momma's last name
4. Result of Marguerite's seduction
5. Attribute of Baxter clan
6. Marguerite's new name
7. Mr. ___ saw his dead wife in a dream
8. His graduation speech made Marguerite angry and sick
9. Mrs. ___ changed Marguerite's name
10. Marguerite's first friend
11. Marguerite drove home from this place
12. What Louise taught Marguerite to do
13. Marguerite described Bailey as her ___ Come
14. Dr. ___ wouldn't treat Marguerite's tooth
15. This title for Momma in court proved her worth and dignity
16. Maya ___; author
17. Owner of the store
18. Marguerite lived here for one month
19. St. ___; Daddy Bailey took children there
20. San ___; Marguerite's home in high school

Caged Bird Fill In The Blank 3 Answer Key

HERO	1. The ___ is that man who is offered only crumbs but is able to make a feast
SHAKESPEARE	2. Marguerite's first white love
HENDERSON	3. Momma's last name
PREGNANCY	4. Result of Marguerite's seduction
LOYAL	5. Attribute of Baxter clan
MARY	6. Marguerite's new name
TAYLOR	7. Mr. ___ saw his dead wife in a dream
DONLEAVY	8. His graduation speech made Marguerite angry and sick
CULLLINAN	9. Mrs. ___ changed Marguerite's name
LOUISE	10. Marguerite's first friend
MEXICO	11. Marguerite drove home from this place
GIGGLE	12. What Louise taught Marguerite to do
KINGDOM	13. Marguerite described Bailey as her ___ Come
LINCOLN	14. Dr. ___ wouldn't treat Marguerite's tooth
MRS	15. This title for Momma in court proved her worth and dignity
ANGELOU	16. Maya ___; author
MOMMA	17. Owner of the store
JUNKYARD	18. Marguerite lived here for one month
LOUIS	19. St. ___; Daddy Bailey took children there
FRANCISCO	20. San ___; Marguerite's home in high school

Caged Bird Fill In The Blank 4

_____

_____

_____

_____

_____

_____

_____

_____

_____

_____

_____

_____

_____

_____

_____

_____

_____

_____

_____

_____

1. Dr. ___ wouldn't treat Marguerite's tooth
2. Attribute of Baxter clan
3. This Baxter was precinct captain in St. Louis
4. It was complete in Stamps
5. Bailey's first love
6. Marguerite's first friend
7. According to Marguerite, he was white but not prejudiced
8. Sister ___ got carried away at church services
9. The ___ is that man who is offered only crumbs but is able to make a feast
10. Uncle ___ was crippled as a child
11. Enviable attribute of whites
12. Owner of the store
13. Marguerite lived here for one month
14. Result of Marguerite's seduction
15. Cut Marguerite in a fight
16. Marguerite's first white love
17. Maya ___; author
18. Momma's last name
19. Powhite___ mocked and insulted Momma
20. Mother Dear; ___ Baxter

Caged Bird Fill In The Blank 4 Answer Key

LINCOLN	1. Dr. ___ wouldn't treat Marguerite's tooth
LOYAL	2. Attribute of Baxter clan
GRANDMOTHER	3. This Baxter was precinct captain in St. Louis
SEGREGATION	4. It was complete in Stamps
JOYCE	5. Bailey's first love
LOUISE	6. Marguerite's first friend
GOD	7. According to Marguerite, he was white but not prejudiced
MONROE	8. Sister ___ got carried away at church services
HERO	9. The ___ is that man who is offered only crumbs but is able to make a feast
WILLIE	10. Uncle ___ was crippled as a child
WEALTH	11. Enviable attribute of whites
MOMMA	12. Owner of the store
JUNKYARD	13. Marguerite lived here for one month
PREGNANCY	14. Result of Marguerite's seduction
DOLORES	15. Cut Marguerite in a fight
SHAKESPEARE	16. Marguerite's first white love
ANGELOU	17. Maya ___; author
HENDERSON	18. Momma's last name
TRASH	19. Powhite___ mocked and insulted Momma
VIVIAN	20. Mother Dear; ___ Baxter

Caged Bird Matching 1

___ 1. LOYAL A. Result of Marguerite's seduction
___ 2. WEALTH B. Mr. ____ sexually abused Marguerite
___ 3. HERO C. Powhite___ mocked and insulted Momma
___ 4. JUNKYARD D. Marguerite's first friend
___ 5. LOUISE E. Johnson children's method of travel to Stamps
___ 6. CULLLINAN F. Enviable attribute of whites
___ 7. GIGGLE G. His graduation speech made Marguerite angry and sick
___ 8. PREGNANCY H. Marguerite lived here for one month
___ 9. KIRWIN I. Marguerite drove home from this place
___10. TRASH J. City in Arkansas where author lived
___11. ANGELOU K. This title for Momma in court proved her worth and dignity
___12. MONROE L. Bailey's first love
___13. MRS M. Marguerite was first Negro to work on the ____ cars
___14. LOUIS N. Owner of the store
___15. DONLEAVY O. Maya ___; author
___16. MEXICO P. St. ___; Daddy Bailey took children there
___17. STAMPS Q. Marguerite's new name
___18. TRAIN R. Uncle ___ was crippled as a child
___19. WILLIE S. Sister ___ got carried away at church services
___20. JOYCE T. What Louise taught Marguerite to do
___21. STREET U. Mrs.____changed Marguerite's name
___22. MARY V. Los ___; Daddy Bailey's home
___23. FREEMAN W. Attribute of Baxter clan
___24. ANGELES X. Teacher in love with information & treated students respectfully
___25. MOMMA Y. The ___ is that man who is offered only crumbs but is able to make a feast

Caged Bird Matching 1 Answer Key

W - 1. LOYAL	A.	Result of Marguerite's seduction
F - 2. WEALTH	B.	Mr. ____ sexually abused Marguerite
Y - 3. HERO	C.	Powhite____ mocked and insulted Momma
H - 4. JUNKYARD	D.	Marguerite's first friend
D - 5. LOUISE	E.	Johnson children's method of travel to Stamps
U - 6. CULLLINAN	F.	Enviable attribute of whites
T - 7. GIGGLE	G.	His graduation speech made Marguerite angry and sick
A - 8. PREGNANCY	H.	Marguerite lived here for one month
X - 9. KIRWIN	I.	Marguerite drove home from this place
C -10. TRASH	J.	City in Arkansas where author lived
O -11. ANGELOU	K.	This title for Momma in court proved her worth and dignity
S -12. MONROE	L.	Bailey's first love
K -13. MRS	M.	Marguerite was first Negro to work on the ____ cars
P -14. LOUIS	N.	Owner of the store
G -15. DONLEAVY	O.	Maya ____; author
I - 16. MEXICO	P.	St. ____; Daddy Bailey took children there
J - 17. STAMPS	Q.	Marguerite's new name
E -18. TRAIN	R.	Uncle ____ was crippled as a child
R -19. WILLIE	S.	Sister ____ got carried away at church services
L - 20. JOYCE	T.	What Louise taught Marguerite to do
M -21. STREET	U.	Mrs.____ changed Marguerite's name
Q -22. MARY	V.	Los ____; Daddy Bailey's home
B -23. FREEMAN	W.	Attribute of Baxter clan
V -24. ANGELES	X.	Teacher in love with information & treated students respectfully
N -25. MOMMA	Y.	The ____ is that man who is offered only crumbs but is able to make a feast

Caged Bird Matching 2

___ 1. DOLORES
___ 2. MONROE
___ 3. ANGELOU
___ 4. VIVIAN
___ 5. MEXICO
___ 6. ANGELES
___ 7. JOYCE
___ 8. LOUIS
___ 9. LINCOLN
___ 10. STAMPS
___ 11. HENDERSON
___ 12. JUNKYARD
___ 13. HERO
___ 14. LOUISE
___ 15. GIGGLE
___ 16. FLOWERS
___ 17. CULLLINAN
___ 18. PREGNANCY
___ 19. KLAN
___ 20. GOD
___ 21. PURSE
___ 22. TAYLOR
___ 23. MRS
___ 24. KIRWIN
___ 25. WILLIE

A. Marguerite drove home from this place
B. Mrs. ____ changed Marguerite's name
C. Marguerite lived here for one month
D. Sister Monroe hit Rev. Thomas with her ___
E. Maya ___; author
F. St. ___; Daddy Bailey took children there
G. Result of Marguerite's seduction
H. Mr. ___ saw his dead wife in a dream
I. The ___ is that man who is offered only crumbs but is able to make a feast
J. City in Arkansas where author lived
K. Dr. ___ wouldn't treat Marguerite's tooth
L. Uncle ___ was crippled as a child
M. Mrs. ____ gave Marguerite the gift of books
N. According to Marguerite, he was white but not prejudiced
O. Searched for a Black man
P. This title for Momma in court proved her worth and dignity
Q. What Louise taught Marguerite to do
R. Cut Marguerite in a fight
S. Teacher in love with information & treated students respectfully
T. Marguerite's first friend
U. Bailey's first love
V. Momma's last name
W. Mother Dear; ___ Baxter
X. Sister ___ got carried away at church services
Y. Los ___; Daddy Bailey's home

Caged Bird Matching 2 Answer Key

R - 1. DOLORES		A. Marguerite drove home from this place
X - 2. MONROE		B. Mrs. ____ changed Marguerite's name
E - 3. ANGELOU		C. Marguerite lived here for one month
W - 4. VIVIAN		D. Sister Monroe hit Rev. Thomas with her ___
A - 5. MEXICO		E. Maya ___; author
Y - 6. ANGELES		F. St. ___; Daddy Bailey took children there
U - 7. JOYCE		G. Result of Marguerite's seduction
F - 8. LOUIS		H. Mr. ___ saw his dead wife in a dream
K - 9. LINCOLN		I. The ___ is that man who is offered only crumbs but is able to make a feast
J - 10. STAMPS		J. City in Arkansas where author lived
V - 11. HENDERSON		K. Dr. ___ wouldn't treat Marguerite's tooth
C - 12. JUNKYARD		L. Uncle ___ was crippled as a child
I - 13. HERO		M. Mrs. ____ gave Marguerite the gift of books
T - 14. LOUISE		N. According to Marguerite, he was white but not prejudiced
Q - 15. GIGGLE		O. Searched for a Black man
M - 16. FLOWERS		P. This title for Momma in court proved her worth and dignity
B - 17. CULLLINAN		Q. What Louise taught Marguerite to do
G - 18. PREGNANCY		R. Cut Marguerite in a fight
O - 19. KLAN		S. Teacher in love with information & treated students respectfully
N - 20. GOD		T. Marguerite's first friend
D - 21. PURSE		U. Bailey's first love
H - 22. TAYLOR		V. Momma's last name
P - 23. MRS		W. Mother Dear; ___ Baxter
S - 24. KIRWIN		X. Sister ___ got carried away at church services
L - 25. WILLIE		Y. Los ___; Daddy Bailey's home

Caged Bird Matching 3

___ 1. MONROE
___ 2. FRANCISCO
___ 3. FLOWERS
___ 4. BLONDE
___ 5. LOUIS
___ 6. GRANDMOTHER
___ 7. LOYAL
___ 8. DOLORES
___ 9. JOYCE
___ 10. CULLLINAN
___ 11. ANGELOU
___ 12. MEXICO
___ 13. KLAN
___ 14. BAILEY
___ 15. JUNKYARD
___ 16. PREGNANCY
___ 17. WEALTH
___ 18. TRAIN
___ 19. MARY
___ 20. HENDERSON
___ 21. LOUISE
___ 22. TRASH
___ 23. MOMMA
___ 24. FREEMAN
___ 25. TAYLOR

A. Attribute of Baxter clan
B. Marguerite's first friend
C. Mrs. ____ gave Marguerite the gift of books
D. Marguerite's new name
E. Johnson children's method of travel to Stamps
F. Result of Marguerite's seduction
G. Searched for a Black man
H. Powhite___ mocked and insulted Momma
I. Momma's last name
J. Marguerite lived here for one month
K. Maya ___; author
L. Enviable attribute of whites
M. Sister ___ got carried away at church services
N. San ___; Marguerite's home in high school
O. Mr. ___ saw his dead wife in a dream
P. Marguerite dreamed she would one day have __ hair and blue eyes
Q. Marguerite's brother
R. Mrs.____ changed Marguerite's name
S. St. ___; Daddy Bailey took children there
T. Marguerite drove home from this place
U. Cut Marguerite in a fight
V. Bailey's first love
W. This Baxter was precinct captain in St. Louis
X. Owner of the store
Y. Mr. ____ sexually abused Marguerite

Caged Bird Matching 3 Answer Key

M - 1.	MONROE	A. Attribute of Baxter clan
N - 2.	FRANCISCO	B. Marguerite's first friend
C - 3.	FLOWERS	C. Mrs. ____ gave Marguerite the gift of books
P - 4.	BLONDE	D. Marguerite's new name
S - 5.	LOUIS	E. Johnson children's method of travel to Stamps
W - 6.	GRANDMOTHER	F. Result of Marguerite's seduction
A - 7.	LOYAL	G. Searched for a Black man
U - 8.	DOLORES	H. Powhite___ mocked and insulted Momma
V - 9.	JOYCE	I. Momma's last name
R -10.	CULLLINAN	J. Marguerite lived here for one month
K -11.	ANGELOU	K. Maya ___; author
T -12.	MEXICO	L. Enviable attribute of whites
G -13.	KLAN	M. Sister ___ got carried away at church services
Q -14.	BAILEY	N. San ___; Marguerite's home in high school
J -15.	JUNKYARD	O. Mr. ___ saw his dead wife in a dream
F -16.	PREGNANCY	P. Marguerite dreamed she would one day have ___ hair and blue eyes
L -17.	WEALTH	Q. Marguerite's brother
E -18.	TRAIN	R. Mrs.____ changed Marguerite's name
D -19.	MARY	S. St. ___; Daddy Bailey took children there
I -20.	HENDERSON	T. Marguerite drove home from this place
B -21.	LOUISE	U. Cut Marguerite in a fight
H -22.	TRASH	V. Bailey's first love
X -23.	MOMMA	W. This Baxter was precinct captain in St. Louis
Y -24.	FREEMAN	X. Owner of the store
O -25.	TAYLOR	Y. Mr. ____ sexually abused Marguerite

Caged Bird Matching 4

___ 1. STREET
___ 2. HERO
___ 3. PURSE
___ 4. MRS
___ 5. SEGREGATION
___ 6. GOD
___ 7. SHAKESPEARE
___ 8. HENDERSON
___ 9. FREEMAN
___ 10. LOUIS
___ 11. BAILEY
___ 12. TRAIN
___ 13. BLONDE
___ 14. FLOWERS
___ 15. LINCOLN
___ 16. TAYLOR
___ 17. GRANDMOTHER
___ 18. DOLORES
___ 19. JUNKYARD
___ 20. VIVIAN
___ 21. MARY
___ 22. JOYCE
___ 23. STAMPS
___ 24. FRANCISCO
___ 25. KLAN

A. Johnson children's method of travel to Stamps
B. Marguerite was first Negro to work on the ____ cars
C. Dr. ___ wouldn't treat Marguerite's tooth
D. San ___; Marguerite's home in high school
E. City in Arkansas where author lived
F. It was complete in Stamps
G. This title for Momma in court proved her worth and dignity
H. Mr. ____ sexually abused Marguerite
I. Cut Marguerite in a fight
J. St. ___; Daddy Bailey took children there
K. Searched for a Black man
L. Mother Dear; ___ Baxter
M. Marguerite lived here for one month
N. Marguerite's first white love
O. Sister Monroe hit Rev. Thomas with her ___
P. Momma's last name
Q. Mr. ___ saw his dead wife in a dream
R. Bailey's first love
S. Marguerite's brother
T. According to Marguerite, he was white but not prejudiced
U. Mrs. ____ gave Marguerite the gift of books
V. Marguerite's new name
W. The ___ is that man who is offered only crumbs but is able to make a feast
X. This Baxter was precinct captain in St. Louis
Y. Marguerite dreamed she would one day have ___ hair and blue eyes

Caged Bird Matching 4 Answer Key

B - 1. STREET	A.	Johnson children's method of travel to Stamps
W - 2. HERO	B.	Marguerite was first Negro to work on the ____ cars
O - 3. PURSE	C.	Dr. ___ wouldn't treat Marguerite's tooth
G - 4. MRS	D.	San ___; Marguerite's home in high school
F - 5. SEGREGATION	E.	City in Arkansas where author lived
T - 6. GOD	F.	It was complete in Stamps
N - 7. SHAKESPEARE	G.	This title for Momma in court proved her worth and dignity
P - 8. HENDERSON	H.	Mr. ____ sexually abused Marguerite
H - 9. FREEMAN	I.	Cut Marguerite in a fight
J - 10. LOUIS	J.	St. ___; Daddy Bailey took children there
S - 11. BAILEY	K.	Searched for a Black man
A - 12. TRAIN	L.	Mother Dear; ___ Baxter
Y - 13. BLONDE	M.	Marguerite lived here for one month
U - 14. FLOWERS	N.	Marguerite's first white love
C - 15. LINCOLN	O.	Sister Monroe hit Rev. Thomas with her ___
Q - 16. TAYLOR	P.	Momma's last name
X - 17. GRANDMOTHER	Q.	Mr. ___ saw his dead wife in a dream
I - 18. DOLORES	R.	Bailey's first love
M - 19. JUNKYARD	S.	Marguerite's brother
L - 20. VIVIAN	T.	According to Marguerite, he was white but not prejudiced
V - 21. MARY	U.	Mrs. ____ gave Marguerite the gift of books
R - 22. JOYCE	V.	Marguerite's new name
E - 23. STAMPS	W.	The ___ is that man who is offered only crumbs but is able to make a feast
D - 24. FRANCISCO	X.	This Baxter was precinct captain in St. Louis
K - 25. KLAN	Y.	Marguerite dreamed she would one day have __ hair and blue eyes

Copyrighted

Caged Bird Magic Squares 1

Match the definition with the vocabulary word. Put your answers in the magic squares below. When your answers are correct, all columns and rows will add to the same number.

A. MOMMA
B. FREEMAN
C. GRANDMOTHER
D. FLOWERS
E. ANGELES
F. TRASH
G. CULLLINAN
H. STREET
I. PURSE
J. SEGREGATION
K. SHAKESPEARE
L. LINCOLN
M. HENDERSON
N. DOLORES
O. MEXICO
P. WEALTH

1. Owner of the store
2. Cut Marguerite in a fight
3. It was complete in Stamps
4. Los ___; Daddy Bailey's home
5. Mrs. ____ changed Marguerite's name
6. Dr. ___ wouldn't treat Marguerite's tooth
7. Enviable attribute of whites
8. This Baxter was precinct captain in St. Louis
9. Marguerite drove home from this place
10. Mrs. ____ gave Marguerite the gift of books
11. Marguerite was first Negro to work on the ____ cars
12. Marguerite's first white love
13. Sister Monroe hit Rev. Thomas with her ___
14. Powhite___ mocked and insulted Momma
15. Mr. ____ sexually abused Marguerite
16. Momma's last name

A=	B=	C=	D=
E=	F=	G=	H=
I=	J=	K=	L=
M=	N=	O=	P=

Caged Bird Magic Squares 1 Answer Key

Match the definition with the vocabulary word. Put your answers in the magic squares below. When your answers are correct, all columns and rows will add to the same number.

A. MOMMA
B. FREEMAN
C. GRANDMOTHER
D. FLOWERS
E. ANGELES
F. TRASH
G. CULLLINAN
H. STREET
I. PURSE
J. SEGREGATION
K. SHAKESPEARE
L. LINCOLN
M. HENDERSON
N. DOLORES
O. MEXICO
P. WEALTH

1. Owner of the store
2. Cut Marguerite in a fight
3. It was complete in Stamps
4. Los ___; Daddy Bailey's home
5. Mrs.____ changed Marguerite's name
6. Dr. ___ wouldn't treat Marguerite's tooth
7. Enviable attribute of whites
8. This Baxter was precinct captain in St. Louis
9. Marguerite drove home from this place
10. Mrs. ____ gave Marguerite the gift of books
11. Marguerite was first Negro to work on the ____ cars
12. Marguerite's first white love
13. Sister Monroe hit Rev. Thomas with her ___
14. Powhite___ mocked and insulted Momma
15. Mr. ____ sexually abused Marguerite
16. Momma's last name

A=1	B=15	C=8	D=10
E=4	F=14	G=5	H=11
I=13	J=3	K=12	L=6
M=16	N=2	O=9	P=7

Caged Bird Magic Sqaures 2

Match the definition with the vocabulary word. Put your answers in the magic squares below. When your answers are correct, all columns and rows will add to the same number.

A. KINGDOM
B. MARY
C. WEALTH
D. LOUIS
E. GIGGLE
F. MONROE
G. GOD
H. STREET
I. DONLEAVY
J. STAMPS
K. HERO
L. PREGNANCY
M. ANGELOU
N. KIRWIN
O. TAYLOR
P. HENDERSON

1. Mr. ___ saw his dead wife in a dream
2. St. ___; Daddy Bailey took children there
3. City in Arkansas where author lived
4. What Louise taught Marguerite to do
5. His graduation speech made Marguerite angry and sick
6. Sister ___ got carried away at church services
7. Momma's last name
8. Enviable attribute of whites
9. Marguerite was first Negro to work on the ____ cars
10. The ___ is that man who is offered only crumbs but is able to make a feast
11. Marguerite described Bailey as her ___ Come
12. Teacher in love with information & treated students respectfully
13. Marguerite's new name
14. Maya ___; author
15. According to Marguerite, he was white but not prejudiced
16. Result of Marguerite's seduction

A=	B=	C=	D=
E=	F=	G=	H=
I=	J=	K=	L=
M=	N=	O=	P=

Caged Bird Magic Squares 2 Answer Key

Match the definition with the vocabulary word. Put your answers in the magic squares below. When your answers are correct, all columns and rows will add to the same number.

A. KINGDOM
B. MARY
C. WEALTH
D. LOUIS
E. GIGGLE
F. MONROE
G. GOD
H. STREET
I. DONLEAVY
J. STAMPS
K. HERO
L. PREGNANCY
M. ANGELOU
N. KIRWIN
O. TAYLOR
P. HENDERSON

1. Mr. ___ saw his dead wife in a dream
2. St. ___; Daddy Bailey took children there
3. City in Arkansas where author lived
4. What Louise taught Marguerite to do
5. His graduation speech made Marguerite angry and sick
6. Sister ___ got carried away at church services
7. Momma's last name
8. Enviable attribute of whites
9. Marguerite was first Negro to work on the ___ cars
10. The ___ is that man who is offered only crumbs but is able to make a feast
11. Marguerite described Bailey as her ___ Come
12. Teacher in love with information & treated students respectfully
13. Marguerite's new name
14. Maya ___; author
15. According to Marguerite, he was white but not prejudiced
16. Result of Marguerite's seduction

A=11	B=13	C=8	D=2
E=4	F=6	G=15	H=9
I=5	J=3	K=10	L=16
M=14	N=12	O=1	P=7

Caged Bird Magic Squares 3

Match the definition with the vocabulary word. Put your answers in the magic squares below. When your answers are correct, all columns and rows will add to the same number.

A. VIVIAN
B. LOYAL
C. GIGGLE
D. LINCOLN
E. TRASH
F. BAILEY
G. TRAIN
H. SEGREGATION
I. LOUIS
J. BLONDE
K. CULLLINAN
L. DONLEAVY
M. FRANCISCO
N. HERO
O. PREGNANCY
P. JUNKYARD

1. It was complete in Stamps
2. Mother Dear; ___ Baxter
3. Attribute of Baxter clan
4. Johnson children's method of travel to Stamps
5. Marguerite dreamed she would one day have __ hair and blue eyes
6. Result of Marguerite's seduction
7. Marguerite lived here for one month
8. St. ___; Daddy Bailey took children there
9. Mrs.____changed Marguerite's name
10. The ___ is that man who is offered only crumbs but is able to make a feast
11. San ___; Marguerite's home in high school
12. His graduation speech made Marguerite angry and sick
13. Powhite___ mocked and insulted Momma
14. Dr. ___ wouldn't treat Marguerite's tooth
15. What Louise taught Marguerite to do
16. Marguerite's brother

A=	B=	C=	D=
E=	F=	G=	H=
I=	J=	K=	L=
M=	N=	O=	P=

Caged Bird Magic Squares 3 Answer Key

Match the definition with the vocabulary word. Put your answers in the magic squares below. When your answers are correct, all columns and rows will add to the same number.

A. VIVIAN
B. LOYAL
C. GIGGLE
D. LINCOLN
E. TRASH
F. BAILEY
G. TRAIN
H. SEGREGATION
I. LOUIS
J. BLONDE
K. CULLLINAN
L. DONLEAVY
M. FRANCISCO
N. HERO
O. PREGNANCY
P. JUNKYARD

1. It was complete in Stamps
2. Mother Dear; ___ Baxter
3. Attribute of Baxter clan
4. Johnson children's method of travel to Stamps
5. Marguerite dreamed she would one day have __ hair and blue eyes
6. Result of Marguerite's seduction
7. Marguerite lived here for one month
8. St. ___; Daddy Bailey took children there
9. Mrs. ____ changed Marguerite's name
10. The ___ is that man who is offered only crumbs but is able to make a feast
11. San ___; Marguerite's home in high school
12. His graduation speech made Marguerite angry and sick
13. Powhite ___ mocked and insulted Momma
14. Dr. ___ wouldn't treat Marguerite's tooth
15. What Louise taught Marguerite to do
16. Marguerite's brother

A=2	B=3	C=15	D=14
E=13	F=16	G=4	H=1
I=8	J=5	K=9	L=12
M=11	N=10	O=6	P=7

Caged Bird Magic Squares 4

Match the definition with the vocabulary word. Put your answers in the magic squares below. When your answers are correct, all columns and rows will add to the same number.

A. MONROE
B. JOYCE
C. SEGREGATION
D. JUNKYARD
E. GIGGLE
F. FLOWERS
G. PREGNANCY
H. MEXICO
I. BAILEY
J. MOMMA
K. TRAIN
L. MRS
M. FREEMAN
N. HENDERSON
O. DOLORES
P. ANGELES

1. Mrs. ____ gave Marguerite the gift of books
2. Marguerite's brother
3. Cut Marguerite in a fight
4. Marguerite lived here for one month
5. Mr. ____ sexually abused Marguerite
6. Bailey's first love
7. Marguerite drove home from this place
8. Johnson children's method of travel to Stamps
9. It was complete in Stamps
10. Los ___; Daddy Bailey's home
11. Owner of the store
12. What Louise taught Marguerite to do
13. This title for Momma in court proved her worth and dignity
14. Result of Marguerite's seduction
15. Sister ___ got carried away at church services
16. Momma's last name

A=	B=	C=	D=
E=	F=	G=	H=
I=	J=	K=	L=
M=	N=	O=	P=

Caged Bird Magic Squares 4 Answer Key

Match the definition with the vocabulary word. Put your answers in the magic squares below. When your answers are correct, all columns and rows will add to the same number.

A. MONROE
B. JOYCE
C. SEGREGATION
D. JUNKYARD
E. GIGGLE
F. FLOWERS
G. PREGNANCY
H. MEXICO
I. BAILEY
J. MOMMA
K. TRAIN
L. MRS
M. FREEMAN
N. HENDERSON
O. DOLORES
P. ANGELES

1. Mrs. ____ gave Marguerite the gift of books
2. Marguerite's brother
3. Cut Marguerite in a fight
4. Marguerite lived here for one month
5. Mr. ____ sexually abused Marguerite
6. Bailey's first love
7. Marguerite drove home from this place
8. Johnson children's method of travel to Stamps
9. It was complete in Stamps
10. Los ___; Daddy Bailey's home
11. Owner of the store
12. What Louise taught Marguerite to do
13. This title for Momma in court proved her worth and dignity
14. Result of Marguerite's seduction
15. Sister ____ got carried away at church services
16. Momma's last name

A=15	B=6	C=9	D=4
E=12	F=1	G=14	H=7
I=2	J=11	K=8	L=13
M=5	N=16	O=3	P=10

Caged Bird Word Search 1

```
F R E E M A N S R L S E L J Y W S R
G J Z J M D R O K O T R O O R I E C
I M R M M E L M J U A A U Y H L G M
G K O H W Y N U P I M E I C K L R F
G M W O A I O N C S P P S E S I E D
L K L T A L C T M E S S M K J E G J
E F J R E X U Y R P K E S R U P A X
R L T G B T L V P A X K L V N Y T R
G J N M Z F L B K I S A V O K V I X
J A M K C N L K C V W H W B Y P O K
M B O P I K I O L F S S K V A A N Q
H A N W K T N B T A D I A D R N L G
G P R E G N A N C Y N E S O D G V W
J I O Y R I N C Q G L R T L S E I N
K Z E G L Z L Y D N M Z R O K L V Q
Z H W E O C R O O F H H E R O E I T
M F Y W S D M D J M S Y E E R S A H
W E A L T H B L O N D E T S W H N V
```

According to Marguerite, he was white but not prejudiced (3)
Attribute of Baxter clan (5)
Bailey's first love (5)
City in Arkansas where author lived (6)
Cut Marguerite in a fight (7)
Enviable attribute of whites (6)
His graduation speech made Marguerite angry and sick (8)
It was complete in Stamps (11)
Johnson children's method of travel to Stamps (5)
Los ___; Daddy Bailey's home (7)
Marguerite described Bailey as her ___ Come (7)
Marguerite dreamed she would one day have __ hair and blue eyes (6)
Marguerite drove home from this place (6)
Marguerite lived here for one month (8)
Marguerite was first Negro to work on the ____ cars (6)
Marguerite's brother (6)
Marguerite's first friend (6)
Marguerite's first white love (11)
Marguerite's new name (4)
Maya ___; author (7)
Mother Dear; ___ Baxter (6)
Mr. ___ saw his dead wife in a dream (6)
Mr. ____ sexually abused Marguerite (7)
Mrs. ____ gave Marguerite the gift of books (7)
Mrs.____changed Marguerite's name (9)
Owner of the store (5)
Powhite____ mocked and insulted Momma (5)
Result of Marguerite's seduction (9)
Searched for a Black man (4)
Sister Monroe hit Rev. Thomas with her ___ (5)
Sister ___ got carried away at church services (6)
St. ___; Daddy Bailey took children there (5)
Teacher in love with information & treated students respectfully (6)
The ___ is that man who is offered only crumbs but is able to make a feast (4)
This title for Momma in court proved her worth and dignity (3)
Uncle ___ was crippled as a child (6)
What Louise taught Marguerite to do (6)

Caged Bird Word Search 1 Answer Key

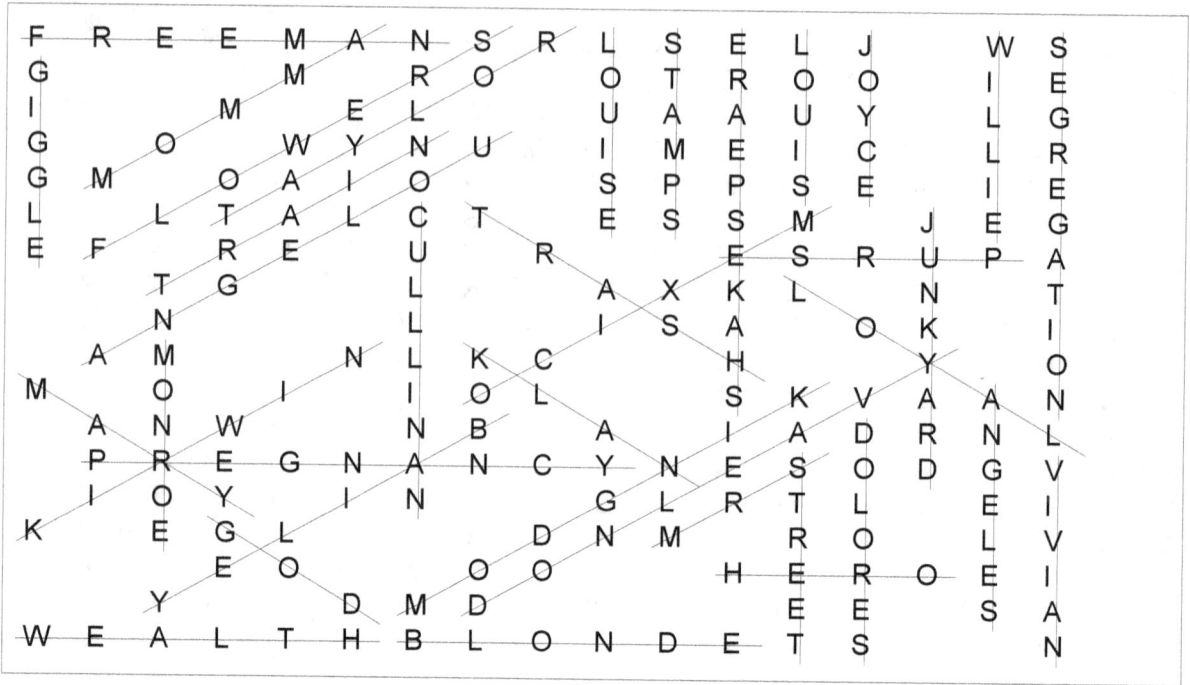

According to Marguerite, he was white but not prejudiced (3)
Attribute of Baxter clan (5)
Bailey's first love (5)
City in Arkansas where author lived (6)
Cut Marguerite in a fight (7)
Enviable attribute of whites (6)
His graduation speech made Marguerite angry and sick (8)
It was complete in Stamps (11)
Johnson children's method of travel to Stamps (5)
Los ___; Daddy Bailey's home (7)
Marguerite described Bailey as her ___ Come (7)
Marguerite dreamed she would one day have ___ hair and blue eyes (6)
Marguerite drove home from this place (6)
Marguerite lived here for one month (8)
Marguerite was first Negro to work on the ____ cars (6)
Marguerite's brother (6)
Marguerite's first friend (6)
Marguerite's first white love (11)
Marguerite's new name (4)
Maya ___; author (7)

Mother Dear; ___ Baxter (6)
Mr. ___ saw his dead wife in a dream (6)
Mr. ____ sexually abused Marguerite (7)
Mrs. ____ gave Marguerite the gift of books (7)
Mrs.____changed Marguerite's name (9)
Owner of the store (5)
Powhite___ mocked and insulted Momma (5)
Result of Marguerite's seduction (9)
Searched for a Black man (4)
Sister Monroe hit Rev. Thomas with her ___ (5)
Sister ___ got carried away at church services (6)
St. ___; Daddy Bailey took children there (5)
Teacher in love with information & treated students respectfully (6)
The ___ is that man who is offered only crumbs but is able to make a feast (4)
This title for Momma in court proved her worth and dignity (3)
Uncle ___ was crippled as a child (6)
What Louise taught Marguerite to do (6)

Caged Bird Word Search 2

```
B L O N D E T E F R E E M A N B D M
V Y G S B V L S H A K E E S P E A R E
A C H W T G H E N D E R S O N M X R
M N Z W G A Y K W X P D S L L L L H
V A G I J R M G A I C M O Z Z C O Q
Y N G E C P E P Q N L M H L S L U C
Q G T J L M S T S P G L F L O P I Z
R E R O P O R J R N N E I M M R S Q
D R A Y K N U J L A Y O L E O R E H
S P I C B R P V I N S L S E T M H S
T F N E S C B V N I W H K R S L M Y
R O L Y A T I E C L M E X I C O V A
E B O O M V O C O L L A R A J R A M Y
E A U Z W R Z M L L R D S L E W T X
T I I L N E X W N U Y Y H L T X I N
B L S O Z G R M V C G X N L Y H A N
L E M N L M O S Z K Y O C R B L X N
Y Y F Z J G D D M O D G N I K D T N
```

According to Marguerite, he was white but not prejudiced (3)
Attribute of Baxter clan (5)
Bailey's first love (5)
City in Arkansas where author lived (6)
Cut Marguerite in a fight (7)
Dr. ___ wouldn't treat Marguerite's tooth (7)
Enviable attribute of whites (6)
His graduation speech made Marguerite angry and sick (8)
Johnson children's method of travel to Stamps (5)
Los ___; Daddy Bailey's home (7)
Marguerite described Bailey as her ___ Come (7)
Marguerite dreamed she would one day have __ hair and blue eyes (6)
Marguerite drove home from this place (6)
Marguerite lived here for one month (8)
Marguerite was first Negro to work on the ____ cars (6)
Marguerite's brother (6)
Marguerite's first friend (6)
Marguerite's first white love (11)
Marguerite's new name (4)
Maya ___; author (7)

Momma's last name (9)
Mother Dear; ___ Baxter (6)
Mr. ___ saw his dead wife in a dream (6)
Mr. ____ sexually abused Marguerite (7)
Mrs. ____ gave Marguerite the gift of books (7)
Mrs. ____ changed Marguerite's name (9)
Owner of the store (5)
Powhite___ mocked and insulted Momma (5)
Result of Marguerite's seduction (9)
Searched for a Black man (4)
Sister Monroe hit Rev. Thomas with her ___ (5)
Sister ___ got carried away at church services (6)
St. ___; Daddy Bailey took children there (5)
Teacher in love with information & treated students respectfully (6)
The ___ is that man who is offered only crumbs but is able to make a feast (4)
This title for Momma in court proved her worth and dignity (3)
Uncle ___ was crippled as a child (6)
What Louise taught Marguerite to do (6)

Caged Bird Word Search 2 Answer Key

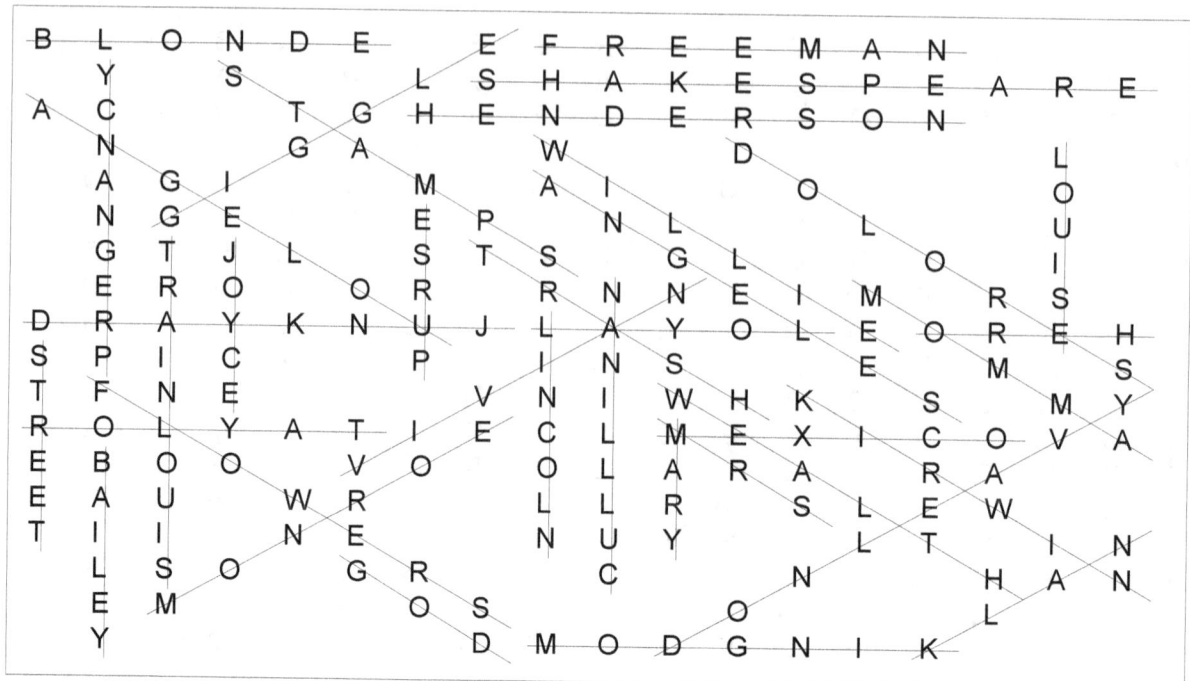

According to Marguerite, he was white but not prejudiced (3)
Attribute of Baxter clan (5)
Bailey's first love (5)
City in Arkansas where author lived (6)
Cut Marguerite in a fight (7)
Dr. ___ wouldn't treat Marguerite's tooth (7)
Enviable attribute of whites (6)
His graduation speech made Marguerite angry and sick (8)
Johnson children's method of travel to Stamps (5)
Los ___; Daddy Bailey's home (7)
Marguerite described Bailey as her ___ Come (7)
Marguerite dreamed she would one day have __ hair and blue eyes (6)
Marguerite drove home from this place (6)
Marguerite lived here for one month (8)
Marguerite was first Negro to work on the ____ cars (6)
Marguerite's brother (6)
Marguerite's first friend (6)
Marguerite's first white love (11)
Marguerite's new name (4)
Maya ___; author (7)

Momma's last name (9)
Mother Dear; ___ Baxter (6)
Mr. ___ saw his dead wife in a dream (6)
Mr. ____ sexually abused Marguerite (7)
Mrs. ____ gave Marguerite the gift of books (7)
Mrs.____ changed Marguerite's name (9)
Owner of the store (5)
Powhite___ mocked and insulted Momma (5)
Result of Marguerite's seduction (9)
Searched for a Black man (4)
Sister Monroe hit Rev. Thomas with her ___ (5)
Sister ___ got carried away at church services (6)
St. ___; Daddy Bailey took children there (5)
Teacher in love with information & treated students respectfully (6)
The ___ is that man who is offered only crumbs but is able to make a feast (4)
This title for Momma in court proved her worth and dignity (3)
Uncle ___ was crippled as a child (6)
What Louise taught Marguerite to do (6)

Caged Bird Word Search 3

```
J M N D J H E N G X X V N D Y T N M G M M M F H X
D P R G K L S L F K L I G B H R A H E K O M C G T
V J B K R F R J X J J V A Q Z A L F D X B M A F S
H P X E S I U O L O U I S M R S K I R W I N M R S
L P R L L N P N F I L A T E R H R X F E I C L A Y
B R L E K M L H W E N N J E G W T R M J E L O V Q
S D Y Y G O G J Y E P C W C D R E R T T M M L L G
F T A K I N G D O M A O O F Q H E L A Y O L A I S
S R R O T R A T H Y L L J L T E S G E I M G G N E
D S R E C O X N A F C S T O N N T R A T N G O H Z
M E S L E E X X C Y T E M H E D A G D T L N G D Q
H L F V S T C T M Y L D H D M E M R O E I V N O F
G E F R P G M Z K W N O N Y P R P F L U H O A N K
S G H B A Z L D D A P O R S C S S S O Y R S N L B
F N G N W N R Q R T L F E N L O W L R Y R S I E P
Q A L N X X C G B B W K F V Q N E L E C Q N L A P
B Q D N F Z R I C Q A V X W J G P V S W P Z L V P
F T R L C B Q N S H N C D D N C J Y J Z T L L Y P
D T Z N V H Q T S C T X T A N Y V S Z T N G U C M
H R R Z X W X K P R O Q X R R Q V H Q T V S C R C
```

ANGELES
ANGELOU
BAILEY
BLONDE
CULLLINAN
DOLORES
DONLEAVY
FLOWERS
FRANCISCO
FREEMAN
GIGGLE
GOD
GRANDMOTHER
HENDERSON
HERO
JOYCE
JUNKYARD
KINGDOM
KIRWIN
KLAN
LINCOLN
LOUIS
LOUISE
LOYAL
MARY
MEXICO
MOMMA
MONROE
MRS
PREGNANCY
PURSE
SEGREGATION
SHAKESPEARE
STAMPS
STREET
TAYLOR
TRAIN
TRASH
VIVIAN
WEALTH
WILLIE

Caged Bird Word Search 3 Answer Key

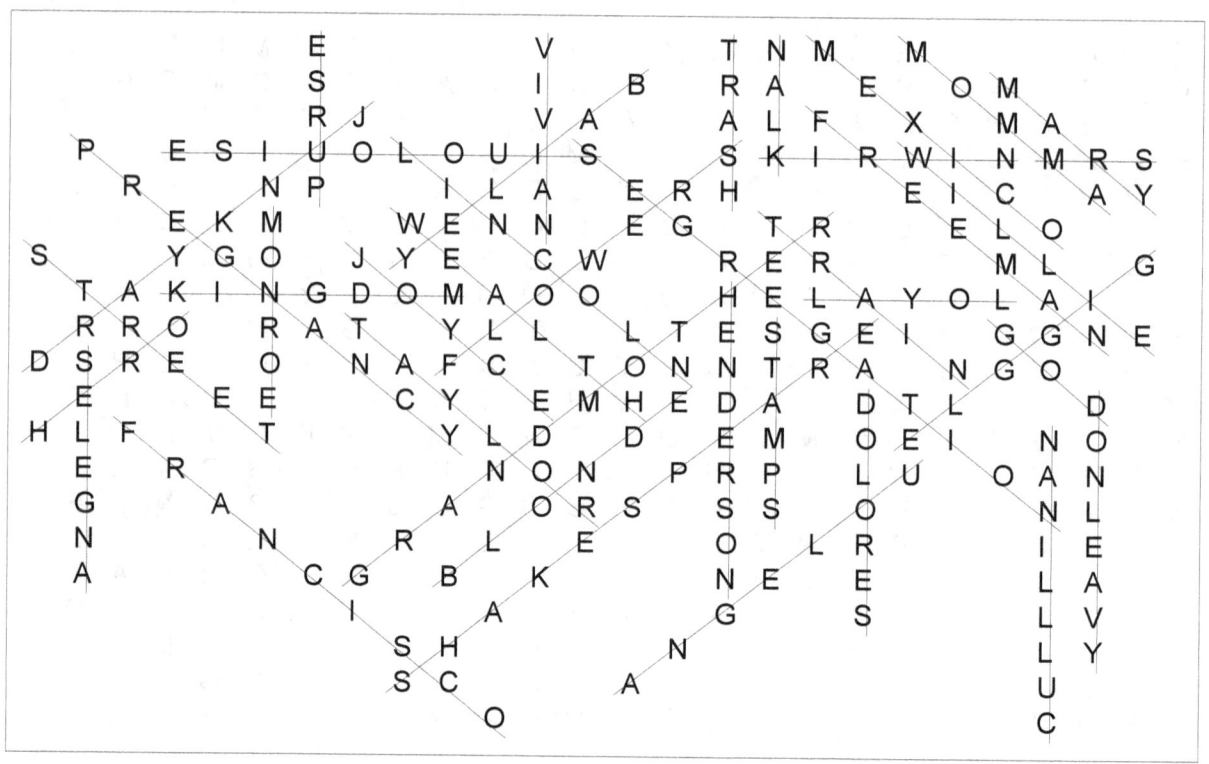

ANGELES	HERO	MRS
ANGELOU	JOYCE	PREGNANCY
BAILEY	JUNKYARD	PURSE
BLONDE	KINGDOM	SEGREGATION
CULLLINAN	KIRWIN	SHAKESPEARE
DOLORES	KLAN	STAMPS
DONLEAVY	LINCOLN	STREET
FLOWERS	LOUIS	TAYLOR
FRANCISCO	LOUISE	TRAIN
FREEMAN	LOYAL	TRASH
GIGGLE	MARY	VIVIAN
GOD	MEXICO	WEALTH
GRANDMOTHER	MOMMA	WILLIE
HENDERSON	MONROE	

Caged Bird Word Search 4

```
A N G E L E S H A K E S P E A R E J R M L Z C T J
N W P Y F Z Z M Q R T X T N B L L K F T D S U G T
G B W N B W R J N D P X V D R X G C S J Q M L R S
E G G V J T L N W X L X R P V V D N K F R Z L A G
L S E G R E G A T I O N X N R G F J X P G G Q L N R
O K D T K J R Q N X S Q Y O K E N M F K J F I D F
U J P H X S W K R X R Q M S T Y G Y H X Y X N M Y
K Y X V P R J I B P E X O R W H M N R Z T Y A O V
L H L C K H M R G C W N N E G V Q Q A R R J N T S
I W A W E L C W F S O T R D X N Q Y A N T M Y H W
N G Y R G L A I Q M L V O N S V V I R N C R A E M
C J O C S I C N A R F R E E M A N J U N K Y A R D
O M L D L Q A G W S X S R H E O O P G B E L O S Y
L S W C R I J R Q S I O N L L Y M T S L T L T M H
N J V B V P G G E U L M N N C N Z M I H Y E O B X
S R Z I L E K L O O W O E E N C W A A A E D Y R X
V P V N S Y G L D L D Y Z X W C B B T R G G V R B
N D J R G G H G J V T Y J G I B S S T N Y T M W K
D Z U Q I S T A M P S X Z H V C K S I C Y C H N F
V P M G M L O U I S B L O N D E O K W I L L I E Y
```

ANGELES	HERO	MRS
ANGELOU	JOYCE	PREGNANCY
BAILEY	JUNKYARD	PURSE
BLONDE	KINGDOM	SEGREGATION
CULLLINAN	KIRWIN	SHAKESPEARE
DOLORES	KLAN	STAMPS
DONLEAVY	LINCOLN	STREET
FLOWERS	LOUIS	TAYLOR
FRANCISCO	LOUISE	TRAIN
FREEMAN	LOYAL	TRASH
GIGGLE	MARY	VIVIAN
GOD	MEXICO	WEALTH
GRANDMOTHER	MOMMA	WILLIE
HENDERSON	MONROE	

Caged Bird Word Search 4 Answer Key

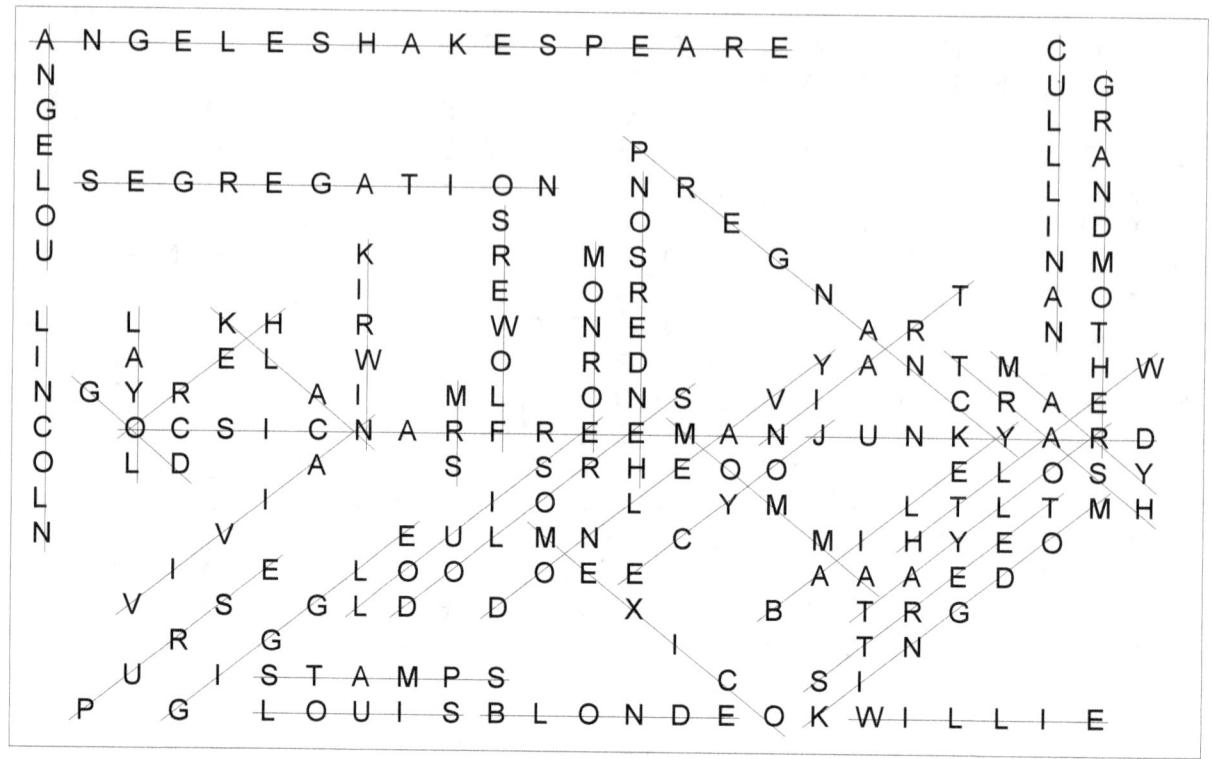

ANGELES	HERO	MRS
ANGELOU	JOYCE	PREGNANCY
BAILEY	JUNKYARD	PURSE
BLONDE	KINGDOM	SEGREGATION
CULLLINAN	KIRWIN	SHAKESPEARE
DOLORES	KLAN	STAMPS
DONLEAVY	LINCOLN	STREET
FLOWERS	LOUIS	TAYLOR
FRANCISCO	LOUISE	TRAIN
FREEMAN	LOYAL	TRASH
GIGGLE	MARY	VIVIAN
GOD	MEXICO	WEALTH
GRANDMOTHER	MOMMA	WILLIE
HENDERSON	MONROE	

Caged Bird Crossword 1

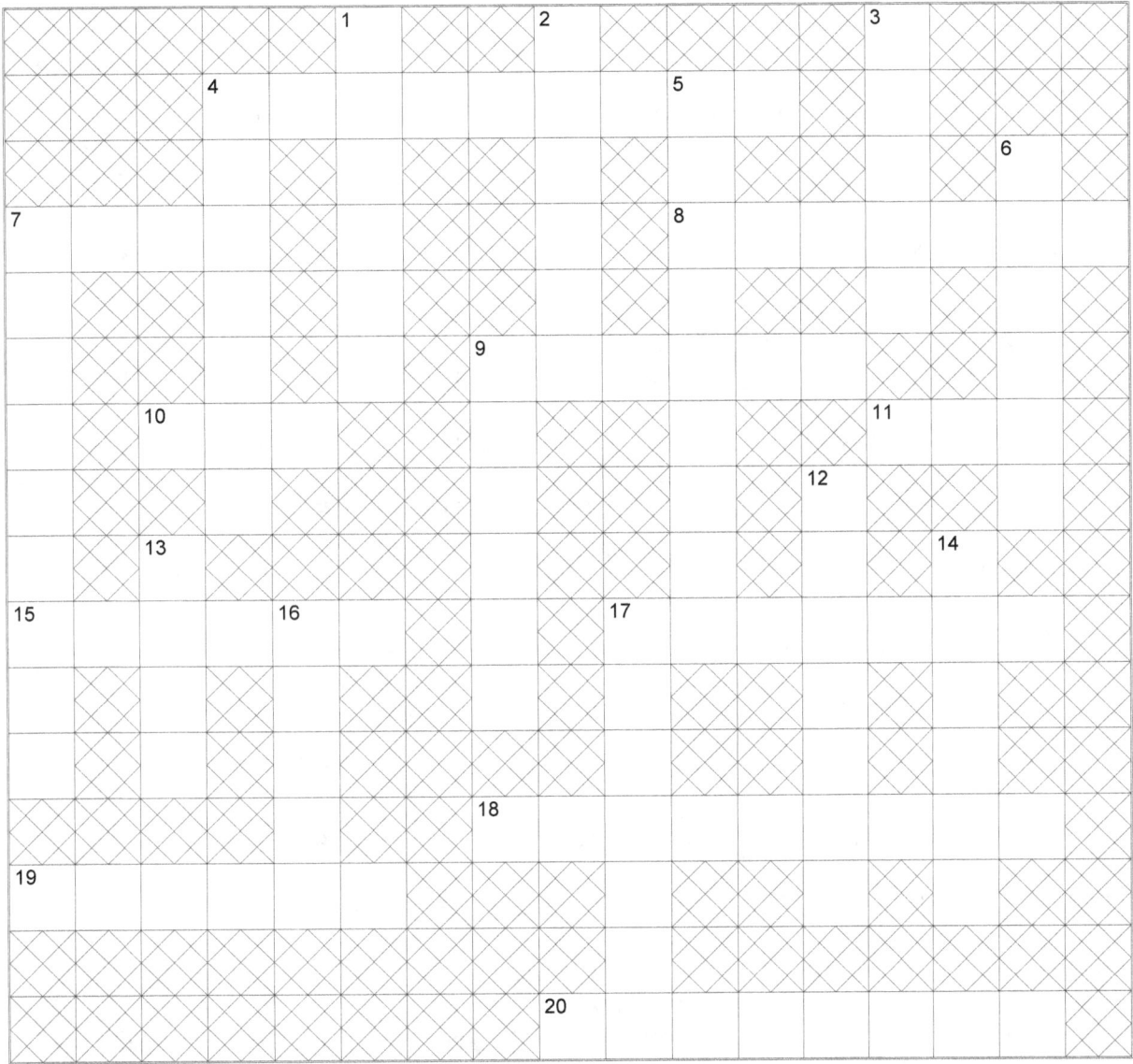

Across
4. San ___; Marguerite's home in high school
7. The ___ is that man who is offered only crumbs but is able to make a feast
8. Dr. ___ wouldn't treat Marguerite's tooth
9. Enviable attribute of whites
10. This title for Momma in court proved her worth and dignity
11. According to Marguerite, he was white but not prejudiced
15. City in Arkansas where author lived
17. Los ___; Daddy Bailey's home
18. Result of Marguerite's seduction
19. Marguerite was first Negro to work on the ____ cars
20. Marguerite lived here for one month

Down
1. Marguerite's brother
2. What Louise taught Marguerite to do
3. Bailey's first love
4. Mrs. ____ gave Marguerite the gift of books
5. Mrs.____changed Marguerite's name
6. Marguerite dreamed she would one day have __ hair and blue eyes
7. Momma's last name
9. Uncle ___ was crippled as a child
12. Mr. ____ sexually abused Marguerite
13. Marguerite's new name
14. Marguerite drove home from this place
16. Sister Monroe hit Rev. Thomas with her ___
17. Maya ___; author

Caged Bird Crossword 1 Answer Key

				1 B		2 G			3 J		
		4 F	R	A	N	C	I	5 S	C	O	
			L	I		G		C		Y	6 B
7 H	E	R	O	L		G		8 L	I	N	C	O	L	N
E			W	E		L		L		E	O
N			E	Y		9 W	E	A	L	T	H		N
D		10 M	R	S		I		I			11 G	O	D
E		S				L		N		12 F			E
R		13 M				L		A		R		14 M	
15 S	T	A	M	16 P	S		17 A	N	G	E	L	E	S
O		R		U			E		N			E		X
N		Y		R			G			E		M		I
				S		18 P	R	E	G	N	A	N	C	Y
19 S	T	R	E	E	T		L			N		O	
							O						
					20 J	U	N	K	Y	A	R	D	

Across
- 4. San ___; Marguerite's home in high school
- 7. The ___ is that man who is offered only crumbs but is able to make a feast
- 8. Dr. ___ wouldn't treat Marguerite's tooth
- 9. Enviable attribute of whites
- 10. This title for Momma in court proved her worth and dignity
- 11. According to Marguerite, he was white but not prejudiced
- 15. City in Arkansas where author lived
- 17. Los ___; Daddy Bailey's home
- 18. Result of Marguerite's seduction
- 19. Marguerite was first Negro to work on the ____ cars
- 20. Marguerite lived here for one month

Down
- 1. Marguerite's brother
- 2. What Louise taught Marguerite to do
- 3. Bailey's first love
- 4. Mrs. ____ gave Marguerite the gift of books
- 5. Mrs.____changed Marguerite's name
- 6. Marguerite dreamed she would one day have ___ hair and blue eyes
- 7. Momma's last name
- 9. Uncle ___ was crippled as a child
- 12. Mr. ____ sexually abused Marguerite
- 13. Marguerite's new name
- 14. Marguerite drove home from this place
- 16. Sister Monroe hit Rev. Thomas with her ___
- 17. Maya ___; author

Caged Bird Crossword 2

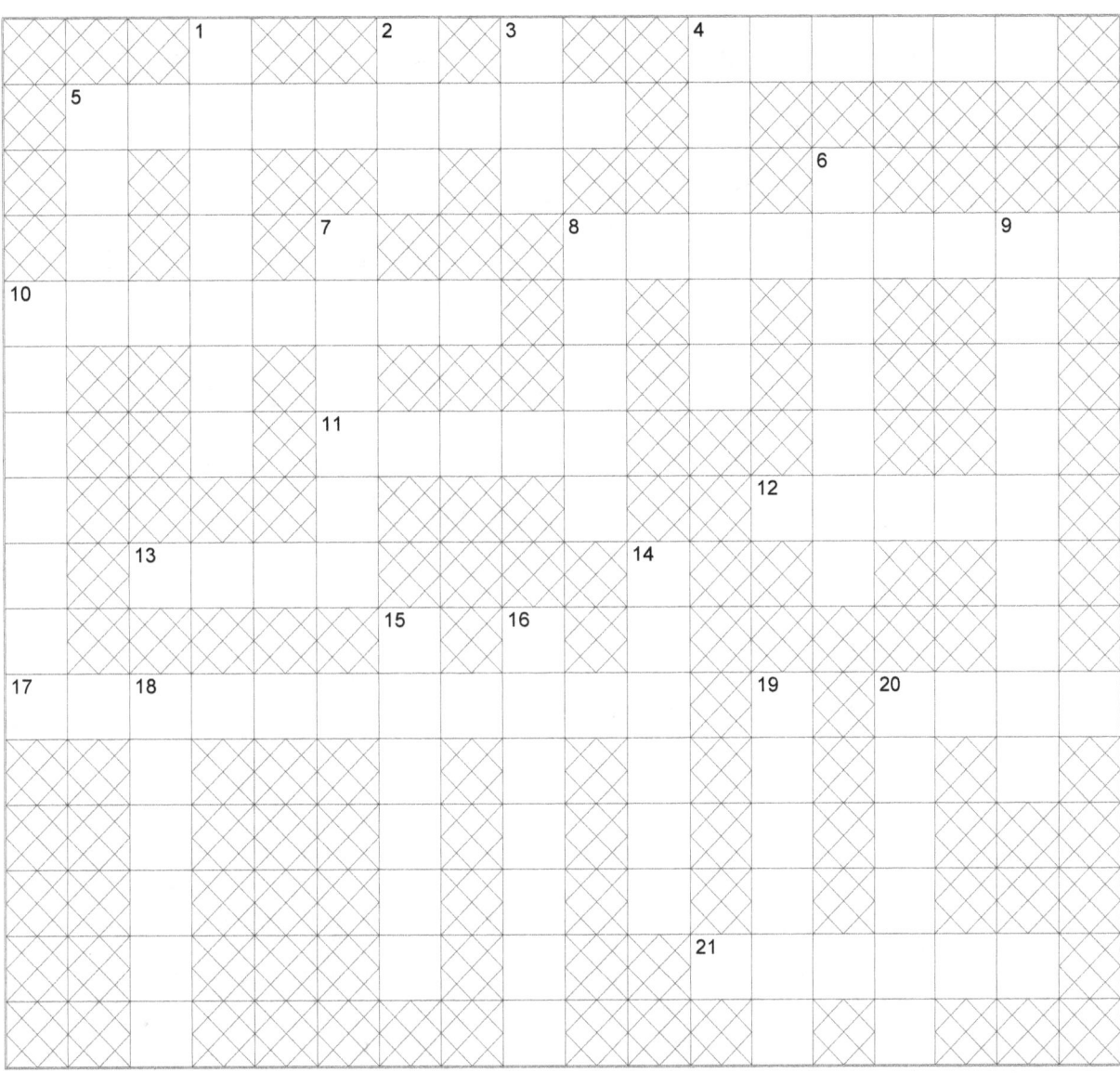

Across
4. City in Arkansas where author lived
5. Momma's last name
8. Result of Marguerite's seduction
10. His graduation speech made Marguerite angry and sick
11. St. ___; Daddy Bailey took children there
12. Attribute of Baxter clan
13. Marguerite's new name
17. It was complete in Stamps
20. Searched for a Black man
21. Mother Dear; ___ Baxter

Down
1. Los ___; Daddy Bailey's home
2. This title for Momma in court proved her worth and dignity
3. According to Marguerite, he was white but not prejudiced
4. Marguerite was first Negro to work on the ____ cars
5. The ___ is that man who is offered only crumbs but is able to make a feast
6. Maya ___; author
7. Marguerite's brother
8. Sister Monroe hit Rev. Thomas with her ___
9. Mrs.____changed Marguerite's name
10. Cut Marguerite in a fight
14. Sister ___ got carried away at church services
15. Mr. ___ saw his dead wife in a dream
16. Marguerite described Bailey as her ___ Come
18. What Louise taught Marguerite to do
19. Uncle ___ was crippled as a child
20. Teacher in love with information & treated students respectfully

Caged Bird Crossword 2 Answer Key

			1 A		2 M		3 G		4 S	T	A	M	P	S
		5 H	E	N	D	E	R	S	O	N				
			E		G		S		D		T		6 A	
			R		E	7 B		8 P	R	E	G	N	A	N	C Y
10 D	O	N	L	E	A	V	Y		U		E		G		U
O			E			I			R		T		E		L
L			S		11 L	O	U	I	S				L		L
O						E			S			12 L	O	Y	A L
R		13 M	A	R	Y					14 M		U			I
E				15 T		16 K		O					N
17 S	18 E	G	R	E	G	A	T	I	O	N		19 W	20 K	L	A N
	I			Y		N			R		I		I		N
	G			L		G			O		L		R		
	G			O		D			E		L		W		
	L			R		O				21 V	I	V	I	A	N
	E					M				E			N		

Across
4. City in Arkansas where author lived
5. Momma's last name
8. Result of Marguerite's seduction
10. His graduation speech made Marguerite angry and sick
11. St. ___; Daddy Bailey took children there
12. Attribute of Baxter clan
13. Marguerite's new name
17. It was complete in Stamps
20. Searched for a Black man
21. Mother Dear; ___ Baxter

Down
1. Los ___; Daddy Bailey's home
2. This title for Momma in court proved her worth and dignity
3. According to Marguerite, he was white but not prejudiced
4. Marguerite was first Negro to work on the ____ cars
5. The ___ is that man who is offered only crumbs but is able to make a feast
6. Maya ___; author
7. Marguerite's brother
8. Sister Monroe hit Rev. Thomas with her ___
9. Mrs.____ changed Marguerite's name
10. Cut Marguerite in a fight
14. Sister ___ got carried away at church services
15. Mr. ___ saw his dead wife in a dream
16. Marguerite described Bailey as her ___ Come
18. What Louise taught Marguerite to do
19. Uncle ___ was crippled as a child
20. Teacher in love with information & treated students respectfully

Copyrighted

Caged Bird Crossword 3

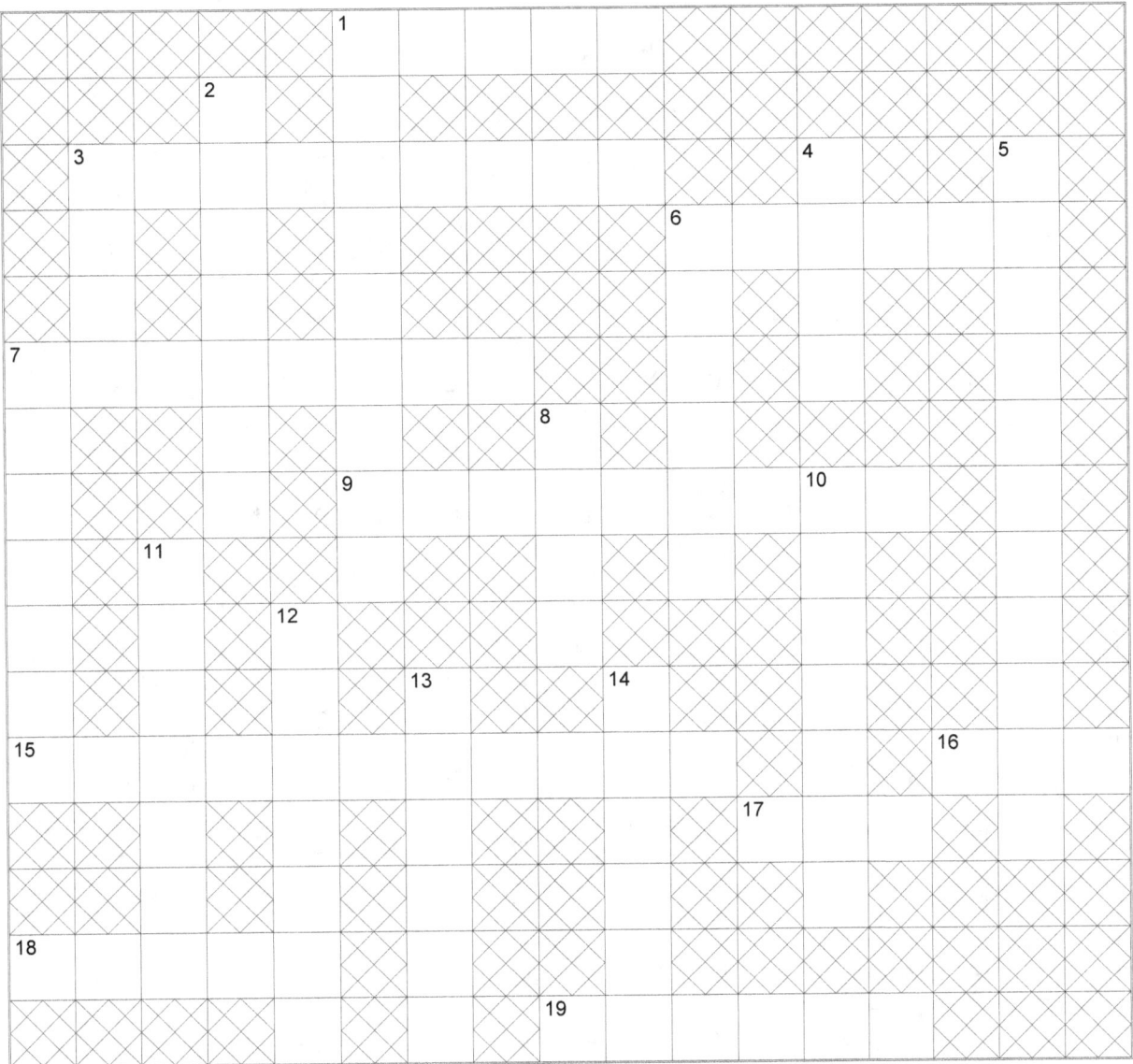

Across
1. Sister Monroe hit Rev. Thomas with her ___
3. Momma's last name
6. Enviable attribute of whites
7. His graduation speech made Marguerite angry and sick
9. Mrs.____ changed Marguerite's name
15. It was complete in Stamps
16. This title for Momma in court proved her worth and dignity
17. According to Marguerite, he was white but not prejudiced
18. Owner of the store
19. Marguerite drove home from this place

Down
1. Result of Marguerite's seduction
2. Los ___; Daddy Bailey's home
3. The ___ is that man who is offered only crumbs but is able to make a feast
4. Marguerite's new name
5. Marguerite's first white love
6. Uncle ___ was crippled as a child
7. Cut Marguerite in a fight
8. Searched for a Black man
10. Maya ___; author
11. Marguerite described Bailey as her ___ Come
12. Mr. ____ sexually abused Marguerite
13. Marguerite's brother
14. Sister ___ got carried away at church services

Caged Bird Crossword 3 Answer Key

					¹P	U	R	S	E					
		²A		R										
	³H	E	N	D	E	R	S	O	N		⁴M		⁵S	
	E		G		G					⁶W	E	A	L	T	H
	R		E		N					I		R		A
⁷D	O	N	L	E	A	V	Y			L		Y		K
O			E		N			⁸K		L				E
L			S		⁹C	U	L	L	I	N	A	N		S
O	¹¹K				Y			A		E		N		P
R	I		¹²F					N				G		E
E	N		R			¹³B		¹⁴M				E		A
¹⁵S	E	G	R	E	G	A	T	I	O	N		L		¹⁶M	R	S
	D		E			I		N		¹⁷G	O	D		E
	O		M			L		R		U				
¹⁸M	O	M	M	A		E		O						
						¹⁹M	E	X	I	C	O			
			N			Y								

Across
1. Sister Monroe hit Rev. Thomas with her ___
3. Momma's last name
6. Enviable attribute of whites
7. His graduation speech made Marguerite angry and sick
9. Mrs.____changed Marguerite's name
15. It was complete in Stamps
16. This title for Momma in court proved her worth and dignity
17. According to Marguerite, he was white but not prejudiced
18. Owner of the store
19. Marguerite drove home from this place

Down
1. Result of Marguerite's seduction
2. Los ___; Daddy Bailey's home
3. The ___ is that man who is offered only crumbs but is able to make a feast
4. Marguerite's new name
5. Marguerite's first white love
6. Uncle ___ was crippled as a child
7. Cut Marguerite in a fight
8. Searched for a Black man
10. Maya ___; author
11. Marguerite described Bailey as her ___ Come
12. Mr. ____ sexually abused Marguerite
13. Marguerite's brother
14. Sister ___ got carried away at church services

Caged Bird Crossword 4

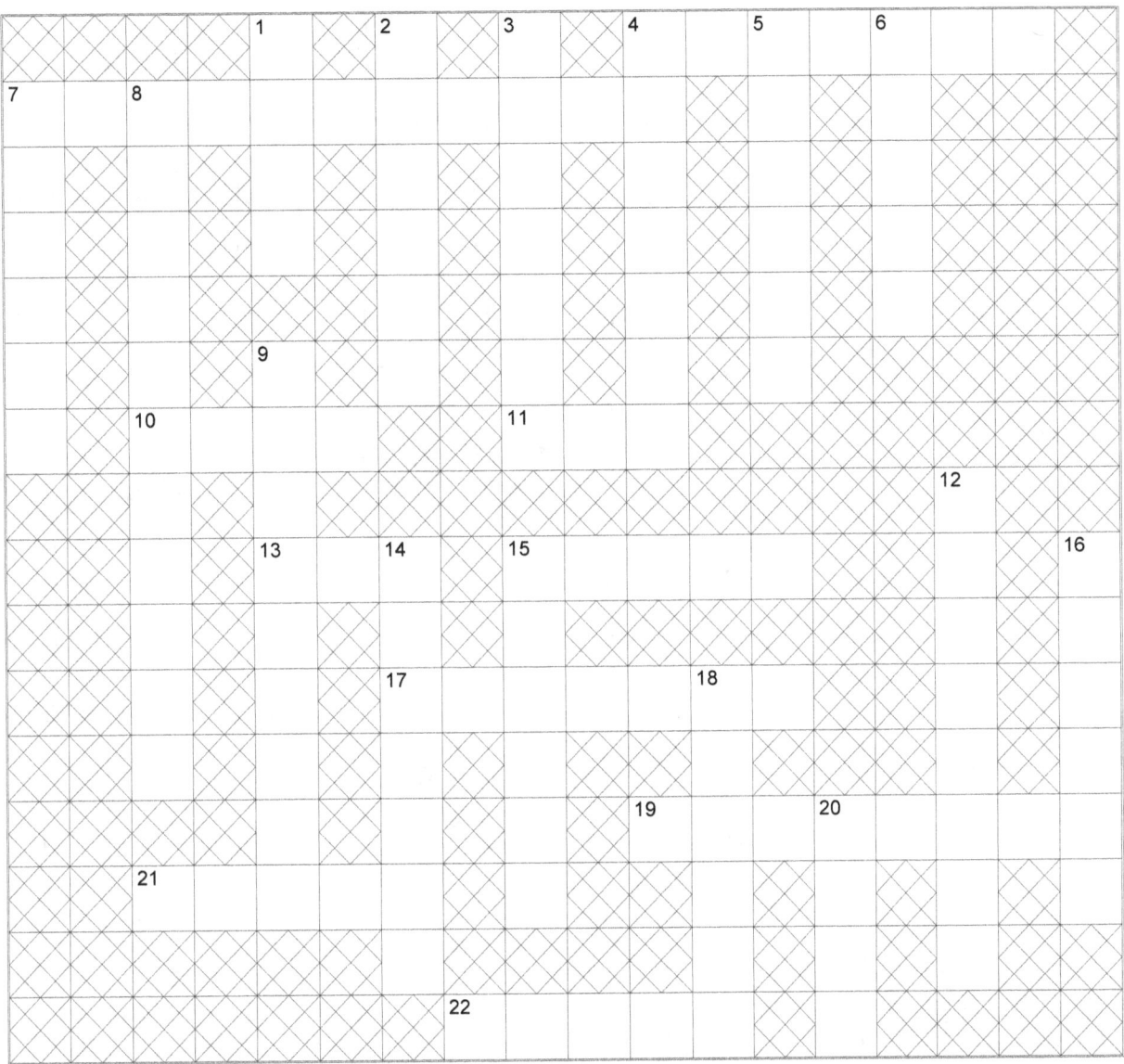

Across
- 4. Maya ___; author
- 7. It was complete in Stamps
- 10. Marguerite's new name
- 11. This title for Momma in court proved her worth and dignity
- 13. According to Marguerite, he was white but not prejudiced
- 15. Owner of the store
- 17. Dr. ___ wouldn't treat Marguerite's tooth
- 19. Marguerite lived here for one month
- 21. Bailey's first love
- 22. Sister Monroe hit Rev. Thomas with her ___

Down
- 1. The ___ is that man who is offered only crumbs but is able to make a feast
- 2. Marguerite's brother
- 3. Marguerite described Bailey as her ___ Come
- 4. Los ___; Daddy Bailey's home
- 5. What Louise taught Marguerite to do
- 6. St. ___; Daddy Bailey took children there
- 7. Marguerite was first Negro to work on the ___ cars
- 8. This Baxter was precinct captain in St. Louis
- 9. Result of Marguerite's seduction
- 12. His graduation speech made Marguerite angry and sick
- 14. Cut Marguerite in a fight
- 15. Sister ___ got carried away at church services
- 16. Marguerite dreamed she would one day have ___ hair and blue eyes
- 18. Marguerite's first friend
- 20. Searched for a Black man

Caged Bird Crossword 4 Answer Key

			1 H		2 B		3 K		4 A	N	5 G	E	6 L	O	U
7 S	E	8 G	R	E	G	A	T	I	O	N		I		O	
T		R	R		I		N		G		G		U		
R		A	O		L		G		E		G		I		
E		N			E		D		L		L		S		
E		D	9 P		Y		O		E		E				
T		10 M	A	R	Y		11 M	R	S					12 D	
		O		E											
		T		13 G	14 O	D		15 M	O	M	M	A		O	16 B
		H		N		O		O						N	L
		E		A		17 L	I	N	C	O	18 L	N		L	O
		R		N		O		R			O			E	N
				C		R		O		19 J	U	N	20 K	Y	A	R	D
		21 J	O	Y	C	E		E		I		L		V	E
						S				S		A		Y	
							22 P	U	R	S	E		N		

Across

4. Maya ___; author
7. It was complete in Stamps
10. Marguerite's new name
11. This title for Momma in court proved her worth and dignity
13. According to Marguerite, he was white but not prejudiced
15. Owner of the store
17. Dr. ___ wouldn't treat Marguerite's tooth
19. Marguerite lived here for one month
21. Bailey's first love
22. Sister Monroe hit Rev. Thomas with her ___

Down

1. The ___ is that man who is offered only crumbs but is able to make a feast
2. Marguerite's brother
3. Marguerite described Bailey as her ___ Come
4. Los ___; Daddy Bailey's home
5. What Louise taught Marguerite to do
6. St. ___; Daddy Bailey took children there
7. Marguerite was first Negro to work on the ____ cars
8. This Baxter was precinct captain in St. Louis
9. Result of Marguerite's seduction
12. His graduation speech made Marguerite angry and sick
14. Cut Marguerite in a fight
15. Sister ___ got carried away at church services
16. Marguerite dreamed she would one day have ___ hair and blue eyes
18. Marguerite's first friend
20. Searched for a Black man

Caged Bird

MEXICO	MONROE	SEGREGATION	TRAIN	GOD
MRS	LOYAL	PREGNANCY	KINGDOM	GIGGLE
PURSE	MARY	FREE SPACE	JUNKYARD	JOYCE
BAILEY	LOUISE	DONLEAVY	FRANCISCO	HENDERSON
STAMPS	SHAKESPEARE	MOMMA	ANGELOU	HERO

Caged Bird

FREEMAN	CULLLINAN	GRANDMOTHER	WEALTH	ANGELES
WILLIE	KIRWIN	STREET	TRASH	VIVIAN
LINCOLN	DOLORES	FREE SPACE	KLAN	FLOWERS
TAYLOR	HERO	ANGELOU	MOMMA	SHAKESPEARE
STAMPS	HENDERSON	FRANCISCO	DONLEAVY	LOUISE

Caged Bird

SHAKESPEARE	BLONDE	LOUIS	JOYCE	BAILEY
DONLEAVY	LOYAL	GOD	CULLLINAN	STREET
MRS	PURSE	FREE SPACE	MONROE	MARY
FLOWERS	DOLORES	MOMMA	WEALTH	LINCOLN
LOUISE	KLAN	SEGREGATION	TRAIN	TRASH

Caged Bird

ANGELOU	KINGDOM	KIRWIN	GRANDMOTHER	FREEMAN
PREGNANCY	VIVIAN	STAMPS	GIGGLE	ANGELES
JUNKYARD	MEXICO	FREE SPACE	HERO	FRANCISCO
TAYLOR	TRASH	TRAIN	SEGREGATION	KLAN
LOUISE	LINCOLN	WEALTH	MOMMA	DOLORES

Caged Bird

KLAN	TAYLOR	BAILEY	MOMMA	HERO
PURSE	HENDERSON	GOD	WEALTH	WILLIE
LOUIS	CULLLINAN	FREE SPACE	FREEMAN	TRAIN
SEGREGATION	FRANCISCO	ANGELOU	GIGGLE	PREGNANCY
VIVIAN	JOYCE	MONROE	TRASH	ANGELES

Caged Bird

KIRWIN	LOUISE	LOYAL	BLONDE	FLOWERS
DOLORES	DONLEAVY	STREET	MRS	STAMPS
SHAKESPEARE	LINCOLN	FREE SPACE	KINGDOM	MARY
GRANDMOTHER	ANGELES	TRASH	MONROE	JOYCE
VIVIAN	PREGNANCY	GIGGLE	ANGELOU	FRANCISCO

Caged Bird

GOD	CULLLINAN	LOYAL	LOUISE	MRS
STAMPS	TRASH	TAYLOR	KIRWIN	GIGGLE
FRANCISCO	PREGNANCY	FREE SPACE	KLAN	WILLIE
BLONDE	VIVIAN	MARY	KINGDOM	DOLORES
MONROE	LOUIS	HENDERSON	MOMMA	BAILEY

Caged Bird

DONLEAVY	HERO	WEALTH	JUNKYARD	ANGELOU
ANGELES	FREEMAN	SHAKESPEARE	STREET	SEGREGATION
GRANDMOTHER	TRAIN	FREE SPACE	JOYCE	PURSE
LINCOLN	BAILEY	MOMMA	HENDERSON	LOUIS
MONROE	DOLORES	KINGDOM	MARY	VIVIAN

Caged Bird

BAILEY	FREEMAN	STREET	HERO	DONLEAVY
MONROE	MEXICO	TRASH	FRANCISCO	MARY
SEGREGATION	GIGGLE	FREE SPACE	JOYCE	MRS
LINCOLN	JUNKYARD	BLONDE	PURSE	WILLIE
TAYLOR	KINGDOM	ANGELOU	ANGELES	CULLLINAN

Caged Bird

PREGNANCY	SHAKESPEARE	TRAIN	DOLORES	WEALTH
KLAN	LOYAL	VIVIAN	KIRWIN	HENDERSON
MOMMA	FLOWERS	FREE SPACE	STAMPS	GRANDMOTHER
LOUIS	CULLLINAN	ANGELES	ANGELOU	KINGDOM
TAYLOR	WILLIE	PURSE	BLONDE	JUNKYARD

Caged Bird

LOUISE	KINGDOM	DOLORES	FRANCISCO	JUNKYARD
GRANDMOTHER	FLOWERS	WILLIE	LINCOLN	ANGELOU
JOYCE	BAILEY	FREE SPACE	STREET	STAMPS
MOMMA	FREEMAN	MONROE	GIGGLE	GOD
HERO	TRAIN	ANGELES	KIRWIN	CULLLINAN

Caged Bird

SEGREGATION	TAYLOR	MEXICO	LOYAL	LOUIS
KLAN	HENDERSON	BLONDE	MARY	WEALTH
VIVIAN	MRS	FREE SPACE	DONLEAVY	PURSE
SHAKESPEARE	CULLLINAN	KIRWIN	ANGELES	TRAIN
HERO	GOD	GIGGLE	MONROE	FREEMAN

Caged Bird

STAMPS	DOLORES	ANGELOU	GOD	HENDERSON
BLONDE	STREET	TAYLOR	FREEMAN	JUNKYARD
KIRWIN	PREGNANCY	FREE SPACE	JOYCE	CULLLINAN
KLAN	SEGREGATION	VIVIAN	MEXICO	MARY
BAILEY	LOUISE	SHAKESPEARE	TRAIN	ANGELES

Caged Bird

WILLIE	PURSE	KINGDOM	WEALTH	FRANCISCO
GRANDMOTHER	HERO	LOUIS	MRS	MOMMA
MONROE	TRASH	FREE SPACE	DONLEAVY	FLOWERS
LOYAL	ANGELES	TRAIN	SHAKESPEARE	LOUISE
BAILEY	MARY	MEXICO	VIVIAN	SEGREGATION

Caged Bird

KINGDOM	LOUISE	FREEMAN	CULLLINAN	KLAN
WILLIE	TRASH	HENDERSON	TAYLOR	GRANDMOTHER
KIRWIN	PURSE	FREE SPACE	DOLORES	JOYCE
LINCOLN	SEGREGATION	ANGELES	MOMMA	HERO
MARY	WEALTH	ANGELOU	DONLEAVY	BAILEY

Caged Bird

STAMPS	FRANCISCO	LOUIS	TRAIN	FLOWERS
LOYAL	BLONDE	MONROE	JUNKYARD	MRS
SHAKESPEARE	MEXICO	FREE SPACE	GIGGLE	PREGNANCY
STREET	BAILEY	DONLEAVY	ANGELOU	WEALTH
MARY	HERO	MOMMA	ANGELES	SEGREGATION

Caged Bird

TAYLOR	DOLORES	WEALTH	STAMPS	TRASH
PURSE	GIGGLE	LOUIS	ANGELOU	SHAKESPEARE
MRS	TRAIN	FREE SPACE	SEGREGATION	VIVIAN
MARY	FRANCISCO	LOUISE	KINGDOM	LOYAL
FLOWERS	MEXICO	JUNKYARD	PREGNANCY	DONLEAVY

Caged Bird

HENDERSON	WILLIE	MOMMA	CULLLINAN	KIRWIN
BAILEY	KLAN	JOYCE	FREEMAN	GRANDMOTHER
ANGELES	GOD	FREE SPACE	STREET	MONROE
HERO	DONLEAVY	PREGNANCY	JUNKYARD	MEXICO
FLOWERS	LOYAL	KINGDOM	LOUISE	FRANCISCO

Caged Bird

STAMPS	TRAIN	LINCOLN	FREEMAN	LOUISE
MOMMA	KLAN	BLONDE	BAILEY	ANGELES
FRANCISCO	VIVIAN	FREE SPACE	FLOWERS	SEGREGATION
TRASH	PREGNANCY	ANGELOU	KIRWIN	GOD
HENDERSON	WILLIE	GRANDMOTHER	GIGGLE	MRS

Caged Bird

MEXICO	MONROE	PURSE	SHAKESPEARE	DOLORES
JOYCE	LOUIS	STREET	KINGDOM	HERO
CULLLINAN	TAYLOR	FREE SPACE	WEALTH	JUNKYARD
MARY	MRS	GIGGLE	GRANDMOTHER	WILLIE
HENDERSON	GOD	KIRWIN	ANGELOU	PREGNANCY

Caged Bird

DOLORES	PURSE	KLAN	MOMMA	STREET
MARY	SHAKESPEARE	HENDERSON	LOUISE	MRS
MONROE	DONLEAVY	FREE SPACE	TRAIN	KINGDOM
CULLLINAN	MEXICO	TAYLOR	BLONDE	VIVIAN
ANGELOU	FREEMAN	ANGELES	TRASH	STAMPS

Caged Bird

WEALTH	GRANDMOTHER	JUNKYARD	JOYCE	PREGNANCY
GIGGLE	LOUIS	BAILEY	KIRWIN	FLOWERS
WILLIE	SEGREGATION	FREE SPACE	LOYAL	HERO
LINCOLN	STAMPS	TRASH	ANGELES	FREEMAN
ANGELOU	VIVIAN	BLONDE	TAYLOR	MEXICO

Caged Bird

LINCOLN	ANGELOU	LOUIS	DOLORES	WILLIE
SEGREGATION	KLAN	STREET	DONLEAVY	LOYAL
BLONDE	FLOWERS	FREE SPACE	TAYLOR	KIRWIN
PURSE	TRAIN	MEXICO	HENDERSON	STAMPS
MONROE	MOMMA	KINGDOM	TRASH	GIGGLE

Caged Bird

HERO	MRS	PREGNANCY	MARY	VIVIAN
CULLLINAN	FREEMAN	JOYCE	GOD	BAILEY
FRANCISCO	GRANDMOTHER	FREE SPACE	SHAKESPEARE	LOUISE
ANGELES	GIGGLE	TRASH	KINGDOM	MOMMA
MONROE	STAMPS	HENDERSON	MEXICO	TRAIN

Caged Bird

VIVIAN	BAILEY	FRANCISCO	TRAIN	FREEMAN
SEGREGATION	MONROE	STREET	CULLLINAN	WILLIE
ANGELOU	TAYLOR	FREE SPACE	ANGELES	MEXICO
DONLEAVY	HENDERSON	LINCOLN	MRS	GIGGLE
KLAN	SHAKESPEARE	PREGNANCY	STAMPS	BLONDE

Caged Bird

GRANDMOTHER	WEALTH	LOUISE	JOYCE	PURSE
KINGDOM	TRASH	KIRWIN	MOMMA	JUNKYARD
DOLORES	LOYAL	FREE SPACE	LOUIS	HERO
MARY	BLONDE	STAMPS	PREGNANCY	SHAKESPEARE
KLAN	GIGGLE	MRS	LINCOLN	HENDERSON

Caged Bird

MRS	BLONDE	KINGDOM	SEGREGATION	KIRWIN
LOYAL	MONROE	MEXICO	DONLEAVY	LOUISE
ANGELES	FLOWERS	FREE SPACE	DOLORES	CULLLINAN
MARY	TRAIN	ANGELOU	HERO	VIVIAN
TAYLOR	FREEMAN	LOUIS	GIGGLE	TRASH

Caged Bird

SHAKESPEARE	KLAN	MOMMA	BAILEY	JOYCE
LINCOLN	PURSE	GOD	STREET	HENDERSON
PREGNANCY	GRANDMOTHER	FREE SPACE	WEALTH	JUNKYARD
FRANCISCO	TRASH	GIGGLE	LOUIS	FREEMAN
TAYLOR	VIVIAN	HERO	ANGELOU	TRAIN

Caged Bird

KINGDOM	BAILEY	PREGNANCY	WILLIE	TRASH
FREEMAN	DOLORES	JUNKYARD	FLOWERS	TAYLOR
LINCOLN	MARY	FREE SPACE	CULLLINAN	KIRWIN
KLAN	LOUISE	MEXICO	MRS	FRANCISCO
GRANDMOTHER	TRAIN	MOMMA	MONROE	GOD

Caged Bird

PURSE	DONLEAVY	SEGREGATION	SHAKESPEARE	ANGELES
LOYAL	HENDERSON	ANGELOU	JOYCE	VIVIAN
WEALTH	BLONDE	FREE SPACE	STREET	LOUIS
STAMPS	GOD	MONROE	MOMMA	TRAIN
GRANDMOTHER	FRANCISCO	MRS	MEXICO	LOUISE

Caged Bird

FREEMAN	LOUISE	MOMMA	LINCOLN	WEALTH
KINGDOM	DONLEAVY	WILLIE	HERO	KIRWIN
LOYAL	GOD	FREE SPACE	BLONDE	VIVIAN
KLAN	HENDERSON	DOLORES	STAMPS	SHAKESPEARE
CULLLINAN	FLOWERS	PURSE	TAYLOR	GIGGLE

Caged Bird

MRS	TRAIN	SEGREGATION	FRANCISCO	JUNKYARD
MONROE	BAILEY	MEXICO	MARY	TRASH
ANGELOU	STREET	FREE SPACE	JOYCE	PREGNANCY
GRANDMOTHER	GIGGLE	TAYLOR	PURSE	FLOWERS
CULLLINAN	SHAKESPEARE	STAMPS	DOLORES	HENDERSON

I Know Why The Caged Bird Sings Vocabulary Word List

No.	Word	Clue/Definition
1.	ABET	To encourage or help
2.	ADMONISHED	Gently reproved
3.	ANACHRONISM	Out of proper or chronological order
4.	APERTURES	Openings
5.	APHORISMS	Brief statements of principles
6.	APPELLATIONS	Names, titles, or designations
7.	APPROBATION	An expression of warm approval; praise
8.	BLASPHEMOUS	Speaking irreverently of a sacred entity
9.	BOURGEOISIE	The middle class
10.	CACOPHONY	Jarring, discordant sound
11.	CAJOLED	Urged gently
12.	CAPRICIOUSNESS	Impulsiveness
13.	COHERENT	Sticking together
14.	COMMENSURATE	Of the same size or proportion
15.	CONDESCENSION	Acting in a patronizingly superior way
16.	CYNIC	One who believes others are selfish
17.	DEBUTANTE	A young woman entering society
18.	DEFERENTIAL	Courteous, respectful
19.	DEFTNESS	Quickness; skillfulness
20.	DESICCATED	Dried out, arid
21.	DEXTEROUS	Mentally skillful
22.	DIABOLICAL	Characteristic of the devil
23.	DISSIPATE	To drive away; disperse
24.	DROLL	Amusingly odd
25.	ECUMENICAL	Promoting unity among religions
26.	ELOCUTION	Public speaking
27.	EMBEZZLE	To take money or property and violate a trust
28.	ENIGMA	Something puzzling or inexplicable
29.	ESTHETIC	Appreciating beauty
30.	EXCRUCIATING	Intensely painful
31.	EXPEDITIOUS	Done with speed and efficiency
32.	FLAMBOYANT	Highly elaborate, showy
33.	FLORID	Rosy colored
34.	FRIVOLOUS	Silly
35.	GAUCHE	Lacking social polish; tactless
36.	IMPASSIVITY	Revealing no emotion
37.	IMPERTINENCE	Boldness
38.	INFUSE	To fill with something
39.	INSCRUTABLE	Difficult to understand
40.	JAUNTINESS	Having a buoyant or self-confident air
41.	LACERATION	A jagged, deep cut
42.	MALAISE	A general sense of depression
43.	MARAUDING	Raiding to plunder
44.	MASOCHISTS	Those who get pleasure from being mistreated
45.	MOLLIFIED	Calmed, soothed
46.	MOROSE	Gloomy
47.	MOTE	A speck
48.	NONCHALANT	Coolly unconcerned or indifferent
49.	OMINOUS	Menacing; threatening
50.	ONEROUS	Troublesome
51.	OSTENSIBLY	Appearing as such

I Know Why The Caged Bird Sings Vocabulary Word List Cont

No.	Word	Clue/Definition
52.	OSTRACIZE	To exclude from a group
53.	PALPABLE	Capable of being touched or felt
54.	PANDEMONIUM	Wild uproar or noise
55.	PARANOIA	Extreme, irrational distrust of others
56.	PERPETRATED	Committed
57.	PLOY	An action done to frustrate
58.	PRETENSE	False appearance
59.	PROVINCIALS	Unsophisticated people
60.	PROXIMITY	Closeness
61.	QUANDARY	A state of uncertainty or perplexity
62.	RANCOR	Bitter, long-lasting resentment
63.	RAUCOUS	Rough-sounding
64.	REBUTTING	Refuting
65.	RECRIMINATIONS	Countercharges
66.	RETRIBUTIVE	Demanded in repayment
67.	SOBRIQUET	An affectionate nickname
68.	SOLICITOUS	Expressing care or concern
69.	SPARSE	Occurring at widely spaced intervals
70.	SUPERCILIOUS	Showing haughty disdain
71.	TAFFETA	A crisp fabric with a slight sheen
72.	TEDIOUS	Tiresome due to extreme slowness
73.	TRAMMELED	Restricted, restrained
74.	TRIBULATION	Suffering
75.	TROUBADOURS	Strolling minstrels

Caged Bird Vocabulary Fill In The Blank 1

1. Gently reproved
2. Sticking together
3. Capable of being touched or felt
4. Highly elaborate, showy
5. Urged gently
6. False appearance
7. Appreciating beauty
8. Mentally skillful
9. Promoting unity among religions
10. Coolly unconcerned or indifferent
11. Brief statements of principles
12. Countercharges
13. Revealing no emotion
14. To take money or property and violate a trust
15. Courteous, respectful
16. Speaking irreverently of a sacred entity
17. Amusingly odd
18. Unsophisticated people
19. Showing haughty disdain
20. To encourage or help

Caged Bird Vocabulary Fill In The Blank 1 Answer Key

ADMONISHED	1. Gently reproved
COHERENT	2. Sticking together
PALPABLE	3. Capable of being touched or felt
FLAMBOYANT	4. Highly elaborate, showy
CAJOLED	5. Urged gently
PRETENSE	6. False appearance
ESTHETIC	7. Appreciating beauty
DEXTEROUS	8. Mentally skillful
ECUMENICAL	9. Promoting unity among religions
NONCHALANT	10. Coolly unconcerned or indifferent
APHORISMS	11. Brief statements of principles
RECRIMINATIONS	12. Countercharges
IMPASSIVITY	13. Revealing no emotion
EMBEZZLE	14. To take money or property and violate a trust
DEFERENTIAL	15. Courteous, respectful
BLASPHEMOUS	16. Speaking irreverently of a sacred entity
DROLL	17. Amusingly odd
PROVINCIALS	18. Unsophisticated people
SUPERCILIOUS	19. Showing haughty disdain
ABET	20. To encourage or help

Caged Bird Vocabulary Fill In The Blank 2

_____

_____

_____

_____

_____

_____

_____

_____

_____

_____

_____

_____

_____

_____

_____

_____

_____

_____

_____

_____

1. To drive away; disperse
2. Occurring at widely spaced intervals
3. Difficult to understand
4. Speaking irreverently of a sacred entity
5. A speck
6. Strolling minstrels
7. Refuting
8. Characteristic of the devil
9. Demanded in repayment
10. Rosy colored
11. Silly
12. Names, titles, or designations
13. Those who get pleasure from being mistreated
14. Coolly unconcerned or indifferent
15. Courteous, respectful
16. Suffering
17. Unsophisticated people
18. A young woman entering society
19. Dried out, arid
20. Openings

Caged Bird Vocabulary Fill In The Blank 2 Answer Key

DISSIPATE	1. To drive away; disperse
SPARSE	2. Occurring at widely spaced intervals
INSCRUTABLE	3. Difficult to understand
BLASPHEMOUS	4. Speaking irreverently of a sacred entity
MOTE	5. A speck
TROUBADOURS	6. Strolling minstrels
REBUTTING	7. Refuting
DIABOLICAL	8. Characteristic of the devil
RETRIBUTIVE	9. Demanded in repayment
FLORID	10. Rosy colored
FRIVOLOUS	11. Silly
APPELLATIONS	12. Names, titles, or designations
MASOCHISTS	13. Those who get pleasure from being mistreated
NONCHALANT	14. Coolly unconcerned or indifferent
DEFERENTIAL	15. Courteous, respectful
TRIBULATION	16. Suffering
PROVINCIALS	17. Unsophisticated people
DEBUTANTE	18. A young woman entering society
DESICCATED	19. Dried out, arid
APERTURES	20. Openings

Caged Bird Vocabulary Fill In The Blank 3

_____

1. Intensely painful
2. Quickness; skillfulness
3. Jarring, discordant sound
4. False appearance
5. Dried out, arid
6. Rosy colored
7. To encourage or help
8. Calmed, soothed
9. The middle class
10. Gloomy
11. Of the same size or proportion
12. Openings
13. Characteristic of the devil
14. A speck
15. Impulsiveness
16. To drive away; disperse
17. Highly elaborate, showy
18. Showing haughty disdain
19. Wild uproar or noise
20. A general sense of depression

Caged Bird Vocabulary Fill In The Blank 3 Answer Key

EXCRUCIATING	1. Intensely painful
DEFTNESS	2. Quickness; skillfulness
CACOPHONY	3. Jarring, discordant sound
PRETENSE	4. False appearance
DESICCATED	5. Dried out, arid
FLORID	6. Rosy colored
ABET	7. To encourage or help
MOLLIFIED	8. Calmed, soothed
BOURGEOISIE	9. The middle class
MOROSE	10. Gloomy
COMMENSURATE	11. Of the same size or proportion
APERTURES	12. Openings
DIABOLICAL	13. Characteristic of the devil
MOTE	14. A speck
CAPRICIOUSNESS	15. Impulsiveness
DISSIPATE	16. To drive away; disperse
FLAMBOYANT	17. Highly elaborate, showy
SUPERCILIOUS	18. Showing haughty disdain
PANDEMONIUM	19. Wild uproar or noise
MALAISE	20. A general sense of depression

Caged Bird Vocabulary Fill In The Blank 4

_____ 1. To fill with something

_____ 2. Names, titles, or designations

_____ 3. Sticking together

_____ 4. Restricted, restrained

_____ 5. Openings

_____ 6. Appreciating beauty

_____ 7. Highly elaborate, showy

_____ 8. Urged gently

_____ 9. Having a buoyant or self-confident air

_____ 10. Occurring at widely spaced intervals

_____ 11. Acting in a patronizingly superior way

_____ 12. Showing haughty disdain

_____ 13. Demanded in repayment

_____ 14. Public speaking

_____ 15. Tiresome due to extreme slowness

_____ 16. A state of uncertainty or perplexity

_____ 17. Calmed, soothed

_____ 18. Suffering

_____ 19. Expressing care or concern

_____ 20. Capable of being touched or felt

Caged Bird Vocabulary Fill In The Blank 4 Answer Key

INFUSE	1. To fill with something
APPELLATIONS	2. Names, titles, or designations
COHERENT	3. Sticking together
TRAMMELED	4. Restricted, restrained
APERTURES	5. Openings
ESTHETIC	6. Appreciating beauty
FLAMBOYANT	7. Highly elaborate, showy
CAJOLED	8. Urged gently
JAUNTINESS	9. Having a buoyant or self-confident air
SPARSE	10. Occurring at widely spaced intervals
CONDESCENSION	11. Acting in a patronizingly superior way
SUPERCILIOUS	12. Showing haughty disdain
RETRIBUTIVE	13. Demanded in repayment
ELOCUTION	14. Public speaking
TEDIOUS	15. Tiresome due to extreme slowness
QUANDARY	16. A state of uncertainty or perplexity
MOLLIFIED	17. Calmed, soothed
TRIBULATION	18. Suffering
SOLICITOUS	19. Expressing care or concern
PALPABLE	20. Capable of being touched or felt

Caged Bird Vocabulary Matching 1

___ 1. OSTRACIZE   A. Courteous, respectful
___ 2. PARANOIA   B. Characteristic of the devil
___ 3. BLASPHEMOUS   C. Showing haughty disdain
___ 4. EMBEZZLE   D. To fill with something
___ 5. TRAMMELED   E. Difficult to understand
___ 6. PANDEMONIUM   F. Sticking together
___ 7. CYNIC   G. Countercharges
___ 8. OMINOUS   H. Gently reproved
___ 9. TEDIOUS   I. To exclude from a group
___10. BOURGEOISIE   J. The middle class
___11. ADMONISHED   K. Extreme, irrational distrust of others
___12. INSCRUTABLE   L. Menacing; threatening
___13. SOBRIQUET   M. A crisp fabric with a slight sheen
___14. TROUBADOURS   N. Strolling minstrels
___15. INFUSE   O. Acting in a patronizingly superior way
___16. RECRIMINATIONS   P. Wild uproar or noise
___17. CONDESCENSION   Q. Speaking irreverently of a sacred entity
___18. DIABOLICAL   R. An affectionate nickname
___19. SUPERCILIOUS   S. Tiresome due to extreme slowness
___20. DEFERENTIAL   T. One who believes others are selfish
___21. TAFFETA   U. Rough-sounding
___22. COHERENT   V. To take money or property and violate a trust
___23. DESICCATED   W. Silly
___24. RAUCOUS   X. Dried out, arid
___25. FRIVOLOUS   Y. Restricted, restrained

Caged Bird Vocabulary Matching 1 Answer Key

I - 1. OSTRACIZE	A. Courteous, respectful
K - 2. PARANOIA	B. Characteristic of the devil
Q - 3. BLASPHEMOUS	C. Showing haughty disdain
V - 4. EMBEZZLE	D. To fill with something
Y - 5. TRAMMELED	E. Difficult to understand
P - 6. PANDEMONIUM	F. Sticking together
T - 7. CYNIC	G. Countercharges
L - 8. OMINOUS	H. Gently reproved
S - 9. TEDIOUS	I. To exclude from a group
J - 10. BOURGEOISIE	J. The middle class
H - 11. ADMONISHED	K. Extreme, irrational distrust of others
E - 12. INSCRUTABLE	L. Menacing; threatening
R - 13. SOBRIQUET	M. A crisp fabric with a slight sheen
N - 14. TROUBADOURS	N. Strolling minstrels
D - 15. INFUSE	O. Acting in a patronizingly superior way
G - 16. RECRIMINATIONS	P. Wild uproar or noise
O - 17. CONDESCENSION	Q. Speaking irreverently of a sacred entity
B - 18. DIABOLICAL	R. An affectionate nickname
C - 19. SUPERCILIOUS	S. Tiresome due to extreme slowness
A - 20. DEFERENTIAL	T. One who believes others are selfish
M - 21. TAFFETA	U. Rough-sounding
F - 22. COHERENT	V. To take money or property and violate a trust
X - 23. DESICCATED	W. Silly
U - 24. RAUCOUS	X. Dried out, arid
W - 25. FRIVOLOUS	Y. Restricted, restrained

Caged Bird Vocabulary Matching 2

___ 1. ENIGMA
___ 2. ABET
___ 3. COMMENSURATE
___ 4. FLAMBOYANT
___ 5. ESTHETIC
___ 6. MASOCHISTS
___ 7. CACOPHONY
___ 8. SUPERCILIOUS
___ 9. DEXTEROUS
___ 10. TAFFETA
___ 11. QUANDARY
___ 12. EXPEDITIOUS
___ 13. ELOCUTION
___ 14. TRAMMELED
___ 15. DISSIPATE
___ 16. DROLL
___ 17. IMPERTINENCE
___ 18. RETRIBUTIVE
___ 19. COHERENT
___ 20. FLORID
___ 21. RANCOR
___ 22. BLASPHEMOUS
___ 23. PROXIMITY
___ 24. PROVINCIALS
___ 25. PALPABLE

A. Restricted, restrained
B. Bitter, long-lasting resentment
C. Done with speed and efficiency
D. A crisp fabric with a slight sheen
E. Unsophisticated people
F. Of the same size or proportion
G. Mentally skillful
H. Demanded in repayment
I. Appreciating beauty
J. Boldness
K. Closeness
L. Speaking irreverently of a sacred entity
M. Amusingly odd
N. Something puzzling or inexplicable
O. Highly elaborate, showy
P. To drive away; disperse
Q. Public speaking
R. Showing haughty disdain
S. To encourage or help
T. Sticking together
U. Jarring, discordant sound
V. Rosy colored
W. Those who get pleasure from being mistreated
X. A state of uncertainty or perplexity
Y. Capable of being touched or felt

Caged Bird Vocabulary Matching 2 Answer Key

N - 1. ENIGMA	A.	Restricted, restrained
S - 2. ABET	B.	Bitter, long-lasting resentment
F - 3. COMMENSURATE	C.	Done with speed and efficiency
O - 4. FLAMBOYANT	D.	A crisp fabric with a slight sheen
I - 5. ESTHETIC	E.	Unsophisticated people
W - 6. MASOCHISTS	F.	Of the same size or proportion
U - 7. CACOPHONY	G.	Mentally skillful
R - 8. SUPERCILIOUS	H.	Demanded in repayment
G - 9. DEXTEROUS	I.	Appreciating beauty
D - 10. TAFFETA	J.	Boldness
X - 11. QUANDARY	K.	Closeness
C - 12. EXPEDITIOUS	L.	Speaking irreverently of a sacred entity
Q - 13. ELOCUTION	M.	Amusingly odd
A - 14. TRAMMELED	N.	Something puzzling or inexplicable
P - 15. DISSIPATE	O.	Highly elaborate, showy
M - 16. DROLL	P.	To drive away; disperse
J - 17. IMPERTINENCE	Q.	Public speaking
H - 18. RETRIBUTIVE	R.	Showing haughty disdain
T - 19. COHERENT	S.	To encourage or help
V - 20. FLORID	T.	Sticking together
B - 21. RANCOR	U.	Jarring, discordant sound
L - 22. BLASPHEMOUS	V.	Rosy colored
K - 23. PROXIMITY	W.	Those who get pleasure from being mistreated
E - 24. PROVINCIALS	X.	A state of uncertainty or perplexity
Y - 25. PALPABLE	Y.	Capable of being touched or felt

Caged Bird Vocabulary Matching 3

___ 1. TROUBADOURS   A. An action done to frustrate
___ 2. SOLICITOUS   B. Refuting
___ 3. RETRIBUTIVE   C. Unsophisticated people
___ 4. IMPASSIVITY   D. The middle class
___ 5. PARANOIA   E. Strolling minstrels
___ 6. ENIGMA   F. Extreme, irrational distrust of others
___ 7. DEBUTANTE   G. Difficult to understand
___ 8. SUPERCILIOUS   H. An expression of warm approval; praise
___ 9. DIABOLICAL   I. Expressing care or concern
___10. EXPEDITIOUS   J. A young woman entering society
___11. ECUMENICAL   K. Names, titles, or designations
___12. RANCOR   L. To encourage or help
___13. ANACHRONISM   M. Rough-sounding
___14. BOURGEOISIE   N. Showing haughty disdain
___15. ABET   O. Out of proper or chronological order
___16. APPROBATION   P. Promoting unity among religions
___17. REBUTTING   Q. Characteristic of the devil
___18. DESICCATED   R. Coolly unconcerned or indifferent
___19. RAUCOUS   S. Done with speed and efficiency
___20. ONEROUS   T. Dried out, arid
___21. PROVINCIALS   U. Demanded in repayment
___22. APPELLATIONS   V. Bitter, long-lasting resentment
___23. INSCRUTABLE   W. Something puzzling or inexplicable
___24. NONCHALANT   X. Troublesome
___25. PLOY   Y. Revealing no emotion

Caged Bird Vocabulary Matching 3 Answer Key

E - 1.	TROUBADOURS	A. An action done to frustrate
I - 2.	SOLICITOUS	B. Refuting
U - 3.	RETRIBUTIVE	C. Unsophisticated people
Y - 4.	IMPASSIVITY	D. The middle class
F - 5.	PARANOIA	E. Strolling minstrels
W - 6.	ENIGMA	F. Extreme, irrational distrust of others
J - 7.	DEBUTANTE	G. Difficult to understand
N - 8.	SUPERCILIOUS	H. An expression of warm approval; praise
Q - 9.	DIABOLICAL	I. Expressing care or concern
S - 10.	EXPEDITIOUS	J. A young woman entering society
P - 11.	ECUMENICAL	K. Names, titles, or designations
V - 12.	RANCOR	L. To encourage or help
O - 13.	ANACHRONISM	M. Rough-sounding
D - 14.	BOURGEOISIE	N. Showing haughty disdain
L - 15.	ABET	O. Out of proper or chronological order
H - 16.	APPROBATION	P. Promoting unity among religions
B - 17.	REBUTTING	Q. Characteristic of the devil
T - 18.	DESICCATED	R. Coolly unconcerned or indifferent
M - 19.	RAUCOUS	S. Done with speed and efficiency
X - 20.	ONEROUS	T. Dried out, arid
C - 21.	PROVINCIALS	U. Demanded in repayment
K - 22.	APPELLATIONS	V. Bitter, long-lasting resentment
G - 23.	INSCRUTABLE	W. Something puzzling or inexplicable
R - 24.	NONCHALANT	X. Troublesome
A - 25.	PLOY	Y. Revealing no emotion

Caged Bird Vocabulary Matching 4

___ 1. ANACHRONISM   A. Lacking social polish; tactless
___ 2. APHORISMS   B. Wild uproar or noise
___ 3. CAJOLED   C. Public speaking
___ 4. RECRIMINATIONS   D. Of the same size or proportion
___ 5. TAFFETA   E. Dried out, arid
___ 6. INSCRUTABLE   F. To exclude from a group
___ 7. DESICCATED   G. Countercharges
___ 8. OSTRACIZE   H. Intensely painful
___ 9. RANCOR   I. One who believes others are selfish
___10. ELOCUTION   J. To fill with something
___11. MASOCHISTS   K. A general sense of depression
___12. TRAMMELED   L. A crisp fabric with a slight sheen
___13. BOURGEOISIE   M. False appearance
___14. DISSIPATE   N. The middle class
___15. CYNIC   O. Difficult to understand
___16. INFUSE   P. To drive away; disperse
___17. FLORID   Q. Urged gently
___18. GAUCHE   R. Out of proper or chronological order
___19. COHERENT   S. Those who get pleasure from being mistreated
___20. EXCRUCIATING   T. A speck
___21. PANDEMONIUM   U. Brief statements of principles
___22. PRETENSE   V. Restricted, restrained
___23. MOTE   W. Bitter, long-lasting resentment
___24. MALAISE   X. Sticking together
___25. COMMENSURATE   Y. Rosy colored

Caged Bird Vocabulary Matching 4 Answer Key

R - 1. ANACHRONISM   A. Lacking social polish; tactless
U - 2. APHORISMS   B. Wild uproar or noise
Q - 3. CAJOLED   C. Public speaking
G - 4. RECRIMINATIONS D. Of the same size or proportion
L - 5. TAFFETA   E. Dried out, arid
O - 6. INSCRUTABLE   F. To exclude from a group
E - 7. DESICCATED   G. Countercharges
F - 8. OSTRACIZE   H. Intensely painful
W - 9. RANCOR   I. One who believes others are selfish
C - 10. ELOCUTION   J. To fill with something
S - 11. MASOCHISTS   K. A general sense of depression
V - 12. TRAMMELED   L. A crisp fabric with a slight sheen
N - 13. BOURGEOISIE   M. False appearance
P - 14. DISSIPATE   N. The middle class
I - 15. CYNIC   O. Difficult to understand
J - 16. INFUSE   P. To drive away; disperse
Y - 17. FLORID   Q. Urged gently
A - 18. GAUCHE   R. Out of proper or chronological order
X - 19. COHERENT   S. Those who get pleasure from being mistreated
H - 20. EXCRUCIATING T. A speck
B - 21. PANDEMONIUM   U. Brief statements of principles
M - 22. PRETENSE   V. Restricted, restrained
T - 23. MOTE   W. Bitter, long-lasting resentment
K - 24. MALAISE   X. Sticking together
D - 25. COMMENSURATE Y. Rosy colored

Caged Bird Vocabulary Magic Squares 1

Match the definition with the vocabulary word. Put your answers in the magic squares below. When your answers are correct, all columns and rows will add to the same number.

A. OMINOUS
B. DEFERENTIAL
C. RANCOR
D. ECUMENICAL
E. CYNIC
F. TRAMMELED
G. RETRIBUTIVE
H. TROUBADOURS
I. TEDIOUS
J. ADMONISHED
K. PERPETRATED
L. PALPABLE
M. FLORID
N. DEXTEROUS
O. OSTRACIZE
P. JAUNTINESS

1. Rosy colored
2. Restricted, restrained
3. Strolling minstrels
4. To exclude from a group
5. Capable of being touched or felt
6. Bitter, long-lasting resentment
7. Menacing; threatening
8. Gently reproved
9. Committed
10. Promoting unity among religions
11. Courteous, respectful
12. Tiresome due to extreme slowness
13. Mentally skillful
14. One who believes others are selfish
15. Demanded in repayment
16. Having a buoyant or self-confident air

A=	B=	C=	D=
E=	F=	G=	H=
I=	J=	K=	L=
M=	N=	O=	P=

Caged Bird Vocabulary Magic Squares 1 Answer Key

Match the definition with the vocabulary word. Put your answers in the magic squares below. When your answers are correct, all columns and rows will add to the same number.

A. OMINOUS
B. DEFERENTIAL
C. RANCOR
D. ECUMENICAL
E. CYNIC
F. TRAMMELED
G. RETRIBUTIVE
H. TROUBADOURS
I. TEDIOUS
J. ADMONISHED
K. PERPETRATED
L. PALPABLE
M. FLORID
N. DEXTEROUS
O. OSTRACIZE
P. JAUNTINESS

1. Rosy colored
2. Restricted, restrained
3. Strolling minstrels
4. To exclude from a group
5. Capable of being touched or felt
6. Bitter, long-lasting resentment
7. Menacing; threatening
8. Gently reproved
9. Committed
10. Promoting unity among religions
11. Courteous, respectful
12. Tiresome due to extreme slowness
13. Mentally skillful
14. One who believes others are selfish
15. Demanded in repayment
16. Having a buoyant or self-confident air

A=7	B=11	C=6	D=10
E=14	F=2	G=15	H=3
I=12	J=8	K=9	L=5
M=1	N=13	O=4	P=16

Caged Bird Vocabulary Magic Squares 2

Match the definition with the vocabulary word. Put your answers in the magic squares below. When your answers are correct, all columns and rows will add to the same number.

A. IMPERTINENCE
B. QUANDARY
C. ENIGMA
D. SOBRIQUET
E. PROVINCIALS
F. MOLLIFIED
G. RETRIBUTIVE
H. SPARSE
I. CYNIC
J. CAPRICIOUSNESS
K. ADMONISHED
L. TAFFETA
M. MARAUDING
N. ABET
O. ESTHETIC
P. OMINOUS

1. Appreciating beauty
2. Impulsiveness
3. Occurring at widely spaced intervals
4. Boldness
5. An affectionate nickname
6. Unsophisticated people
7. Gently reproved
8. To encourage or help
9. Calmed, soothed
10. Something puzzling or inexplicable
11. Raiding to plunder
12. A crisp fabric with a slight sheen
13. One who believes others are selfish
14. Menacing; threatening
15. A state of uncertainty or perplexity
16. Demanded in repayment

A=	B=	C=	D=
E=	F=	G=	H=
I=	J=	K=	L=
M=	N=	O=	P=

Caged Bird Vocabulary Magic Squares 2 Answer Key

Match the definition with the vocabulary word. Put your answers in the magic squares below. When your answers are correct, all columns and rows will add to the same number.

A. IMPERTINENCE
B. QUANDARY
C. ENIGMA
D. SOBRIQUET
E. PROVINCIALS
F. MOLLIFIED
G. RETRIBUTIVE
H. SPARSE
I. CYNIC
J. CAPRICIOUSNESS
K. ADMONISHED
L. TAFFETA
M. MARAUDING
N. ABET
O. ESTHETIC
P. OMINOUS

1. Appreciating beauty
2. Impulsiveness
3. Occurring at widely spaced intervals
4. Boldness
5. An affectionate nickname
6. Unsophisticated people
7. Gently reproved
8. To encourage or help
9. Calmed, soothed
10. Something puzzling or inexplicable
11. Raiding to plunder
12. A crisp fabric with a slight sheen
13. One who believes others are selfish
14. Menacing; threatening
15. A state of uncertainty or perplexity
16. Demanded in repayment

A=4	B=15	C=10	D=5
E=6	F=9	G=16	H=3
I=13	J=2	K=7	L=12
M=11	N=8	O=1	P=14

Caged Bird Vocabulary Magic Squares 3

Match the definition with the vocabulary word. Put your answers in the magic squares below. When your answers are correct, all columns and rows will add to the same number.

A. ANACHRONISM
B. NONCHALANT
C. CAPRICIOUSNESS
D. PALPABLE
E. ENIGMA
F. MOTE
G. IMPERTINENCE
H. EXCRUCIATING
I. TEDIOUS
J. COMMENSURATE
K. PARANOIA
L. DEFERENTIAL
M. RETRIBUTIVE
N. ECUMENICAL
O. COHERENT
P. LACERATION

1. Out of proper or chronological order
2. Promoting unity among religions
3. Of the same size or proportion
4. Something puzzling or inexplicable
5. Boldness
6. Courteous, respectful
7. A jagged, deep cut
8. Impulsiveness
9. Sticking together
10. Capable of being touched or felt
11. Intensely painful
12. Extreme, irrational distrust of others
13. Tiresome due to extreme slowness
14. A speck
15. Coolly unconcerned or indifferent
16. Demanded in repayment

A=	B=	C=	D=
E=	F=	G=	H=
I=	J=	K=	L=
M=	N=	O=	P=

Caged Bird Vocabulary Magic Squares 3 Answer Key

Match the definition with the vocabulary word. Put your answers in the magic squares below. When your answers are correct, all columns and rows will add to the same number.

A. ANACHRONISM
B. NONCHALANT
C. CAPRICIOUSNESS
D. PALPABLE
E. ENIGMA
F. MOTE

G. IMPERTINENCE
H. EXCRUCIATING
I. TEDIOUS
J. COMMENSURATE
K. PARANOIA
L. DEFERENTIAL

M. RETRIBUTIVE
N. ECUMENICAL
O. COHERENT
P. LACERATION

1. Out of proper or chronological order
2. Promoting unity among religions
3. Of the same size or proportion
4. Something puzzling or inexplicable
5. Boldness
6. Courteous, respectful
7. A jagged, deep cut
8. Impulsiveness
9. Sticking together
10. Capable of being touched or felt
11. Intensely painful
12. Extreme, irrational distrust of others
13. Tiresome due to extreme slowness
14. A speck
15. Coolly unconcerned or indifferent
16. Demanded in repayment

A=1	B=15	C=8	D=10
E=4	F=14	G=5	H=11
I=13	J=3	K=12	L=6
M=16	N=2	O=9	P=7

Caged Bird Vocabulary Magic Squares 4

Match the definition with the vocabulary word. Put your answers in the magic squares below. When your answers are correct, all columns and rows will add to the same number.

A. EXCRUCIATING
B. BOURGEOISIE
C. PALPABLE
D. DISSIPATE
E. QUANDARY
F. FLAMBOYANT
G. MALAISE
H. REBUTTING
I. IMPASSIVITY
J. MASOCHISTS
K. FRIVOLOUS
L. INSCRUTABLE
M. ELOCUTION
N. OMINOUS
O. RETRIBUTIVE
P. MOROSE

1. Highly elaborate, showy
2. Revealing no emotion
3. Demanded in repayment
4. To drive away; disperse
5. Public speaking
6. The middle class
7. Refuting
8. Silly
9. Capable of being touched or felt
10. Gloomy
11. Those who get pleasure from being mistreated
12. A state of uncertainty or perplexity
13. Difficult to understand
14. A general sense of depression
15. Intensely painful
16. Menacing; threatening

A=	B=	C=	D=
E=	F=	G=	H=
I=	J=	K=	L=
M=	N=	O=	P=

Caged Bird Vocabulary Magic Squares 4 Answer Key

Match the definition with the vocabulary word. Put your answers in the magic squares below. When your answers are correct, all columns and rows will add to the same number.

A. EXCRUCIATING
B. BOURGEOISIE
C. PALPABLE
D. DISSIPATE
E. QUANDARY
F. FLAMBOYANT
G. MALAISE
H. REBUTTING
I. IMPASSIVITY
J. MASOCHISTS
K. FRIVOLOUS
L. INSCRUTABLE
M. ELOCUTION
N. OMINOUS
O. RETRIBUTIVE
P. MOROSE

1. Highly elaborate, showy
2. Revealing no emotion
3. Demanded in repayment
4. To drive away; disperse
5. Public speaking
6. The middle class
7. Refuting
8. Silly
9. Capable of being touched or felt
10. Gloomy
11. Those who get pleasure from being mistreated
12. A state of uncertainty or perplexity
13. Difficult to understand
14. A general sense of depression
15. Intensely painful
16. Menacing; threatening

A=15	B=6	C=9	D=4
E=12	F=1	G=14	H=7
I=2	J=11	K=8	L=13
M=5	N=16	O=3	P=10

Caged Bird Vocabulary Word Search 1

```
N M P S M A S O C H I S T S P R E T E N S E
O O O R L A N R S Y C S M L F A F N C Y E N
I L N T O Z R K A T C G O X G H L L I S B X
T D S C E X T A R U R Y B V L D Q P O G Y H
A S R M H V I O U C C A N A V V X R A R M N
L E N O G A C M N D R O C I C H O U F B I A
U X X Z L N L S I G I I U I C M C S K T L D
B F F C A L S A S T L N T S Z H S Q S R K E
I G R R R E T U N O Y E G X E E U U T O K V
R P H I N U O E B T H S T B N J O A D U B F
T T A T V R C A D T C E P S M I R N I B O Y
C N F N E O I I S I S A U A L T E D S A U X
T E N T D D L E A I O O J I R L N A S D R N
D R X S W E S O A T I U C O N S O R I O G T
S E Z C V U M L U C I R S N L F E Y P U E W
D H K X O V A O I S E N G S J E U G A R O W
C O F N Q M Y R N P W Q G B D V D S T S I T
M C I L L K P M U I A D M O N I S H E D S L
D M Q J Y A D S T E U Q I R B O S T B F I K
O A N A C H R O N I S M S I R O H P A C E R
```

A general sense of depression (7)
A speck (4)
A state of uncertainty or perplexity (8)
Amusingly odd (5)
An action done to frustrate (4)
An affectionate nickname (9)
Appreciating beauty (8)
Bitter, long-lasting resentment (6)
Brief statements of principles (9)
Capable of being touched or felt (8)
Characteristic of the devil (10)
Closeness (9)
Coolly unconcerned or indifferent (10)
False appearance (8)
Gently reproved (10)
Gloomy (6)
Impulsiveness (14)
Intensely painful (12)
Lacking social polish; tactless (6)
Menacing; threatening (7)
Mentally skillful (9)
Occurring at widely spaced intervals (6)
One who believes others are selfish (5)
Out of proper or chronological order (11)

Raiding to plunder (9)
Rosy colored (6)
Rough-sounding (7)
Showing haughty disdain (12)
Silly (9)
Something puzzling or inexplicable (6)
Sticking together (8)
Strolling minstrels (11)
Suffering (11)
The middle class (11)
Those who get pleasure from being mistreated (10)
Tiresome due to extreme slowness (7)
To drive away; disperse (9)
To encourage or help (4)
To exclude from a group (9)
To fill with something (6)
Troublesome (7)
Urged gently (7)
Wild uproar or noise (11)
Quickness; skillfulness (8)

Caged Bird Vocabulary Word Search 1 Answer Key

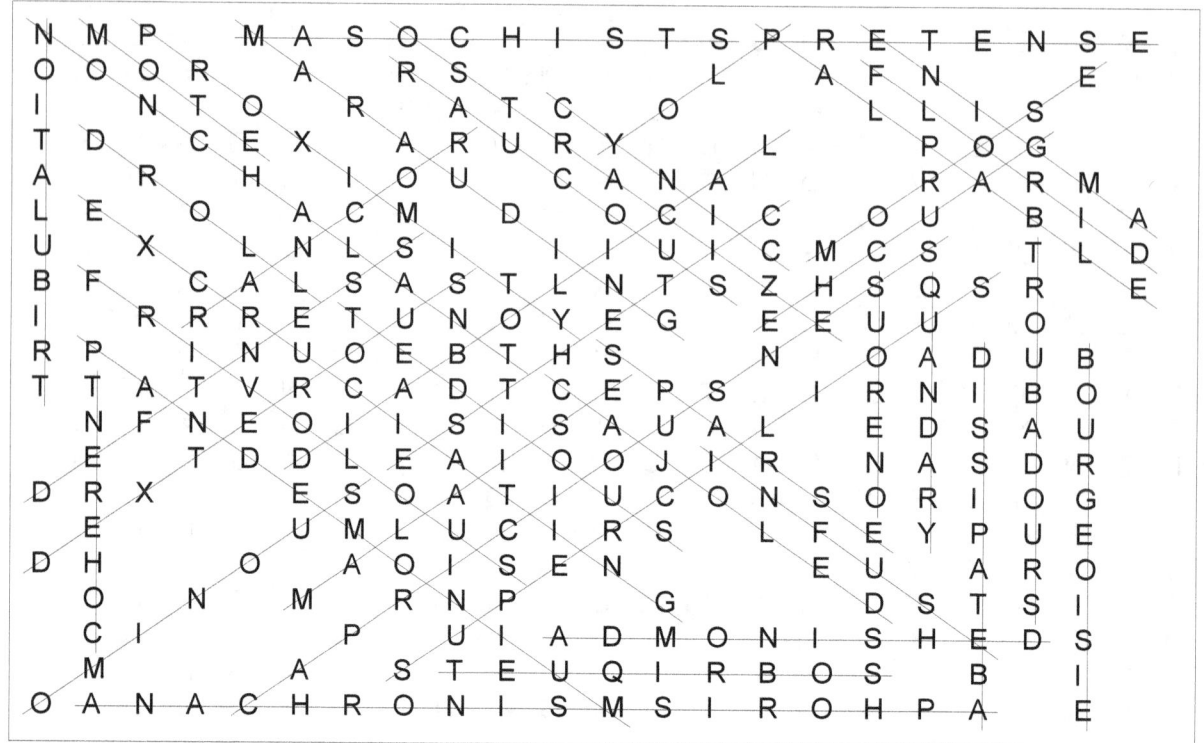

A general sense of depression (7)
A speck (4)
A state of uncertainty or perplexity (8)
Amusingly odd (5)
An action done to frustrate (4)
An affectionate nickname (9)
Appreciating beauty (8)
Bitter, long-lasting resentment (6)
Brief statements of principles (9)
Capable of being touched or felt (8)
Characteristic of the devil (10)
Closeness (9)
Coolly unconcerned or indifferent (10)
False appearance (8)
Gently reproved (10)
Gloomy (6)
Impulsiveness (14)
Intensely painful (12)
Lacking social polish; tactless (6)
Menacing; threatening (7)
Mentally skillful (9)
Occurring at widely spaced intervals (6)
One who believes others are selfish (5)
Out of proper or chronological order (11)

Raiding to plunder (9)
Rosy colored (6)
Rough-sounding (7)
Showing haughty disdain (12)
Silly (9)
Something puzzling or inexplicable (6)
Sticking together (8)
Strolling minstrels (11)
Suffering (11)
The middle class (11)
Those who get pleasure from being mistreated (10)
Tiresome due to extreme slowness (7)
To drive away; disperse (9)
To encourage or help (4)
To exclude from a group (9)
To fill with something (6)
Troublesome (7)
Urged gently (7)
Wild uproar or noise (11)
Quickness; skillfulness (8)

Caged Bird Vocabulary Word Search 2

```
W T D Z F R A D M O N I S H E D C S H A K G
H Z L I A E O M I N O U S D E E R U I B M B
Q P G N A M N Z X V K Y S S T S K C O Y E S K
M S C Q H B Q N Y K L S A R M D N I L T U J
D O M O T E O T J B E C A S E A G D P L O Y
R B R H B Z H L I N C P U L R N N E T N T V
F R C O J Z S S I I S O O A P A I T R O I S
L I Y E S L N T S C L J P I R C T G A I C L
O Q N F C E N E J O A P R C O H T N M T I Q
R U I G T U D Q V C E L E N X R U I M A L H
I E C S A L M I Y L K S T I I O B T E L O W
D T O J H U R E L M E U E V M N E A L U S M
E P A D E F C A N Z Y O N O I I R I E B S Y
I A N F V S T H I I Z C S R T S J C D I E R
F L D Z F I T C E W C U E P Y M P U I R N L
I P H X O E A H Q T O A C G G J P R N T B
L A X N K R T N E R Y R L Y Z W Y C F P F B
L B S B T J V A E T N E R E H O C X U Y E B
O L B S M E C N E N I T R E P M I E S N D R
M E O P G P O B E L O C U T I O N S E Q W X
```

- A crisp fabric with a slight sheen (7)
- A speck (4)
- Amusingly odd (5)
- An action done to frustrate (4)
- An affectionate nickname (9)
- Appearing as such (10)
- Appreciating beauty (8)
- Bitter, long-lasting resentment (6)
- Boldness (12)
- Calmed, soothed (9)
- Capable of being touched or felt (8)
- Characteristic of the devil (10)
- Closeness (9)
- Dried out, arid (10)
- Expressing care or concern (10)
- Extreme, irrational distrust of others (8)
- False appearance (8)
- Gently reproved (10)
- Gloomy (6)
- Having a buoyant or self-confident air (10)
- Intensely painful (12)
- Lacking social polish; tactless (6)
- Menacing; threatening (7)
- Names, titles, or designations (12)
- Occurring at widely spaced intervals (6)
- One who believes others are selfish (5)
- Out of proper or chronological order (11)
- Promoting unity among religions (10)
- Public speaking (9)
- Refuting (9)
- Restricted, restrained (9)
- Rosy colored (6)
- Rough-sounding (7)
- Silly (9)
- Something puzzling or inexplicable (6)
- Sticking together (8)
- Suffering (11)
- Tiresome due to extreme slowness (7)
- To encourage or help (4)
- To exclude from a group (9)
- To fill with something (6)
- To take money or property and violate a trust (8)
- Troublesome (7)
- Unsophisticated people (11)
- Urged gently (7)
- Quickness; skillfulness (8)

Caged Bird Vocabulary Word Search 2 Answer Key

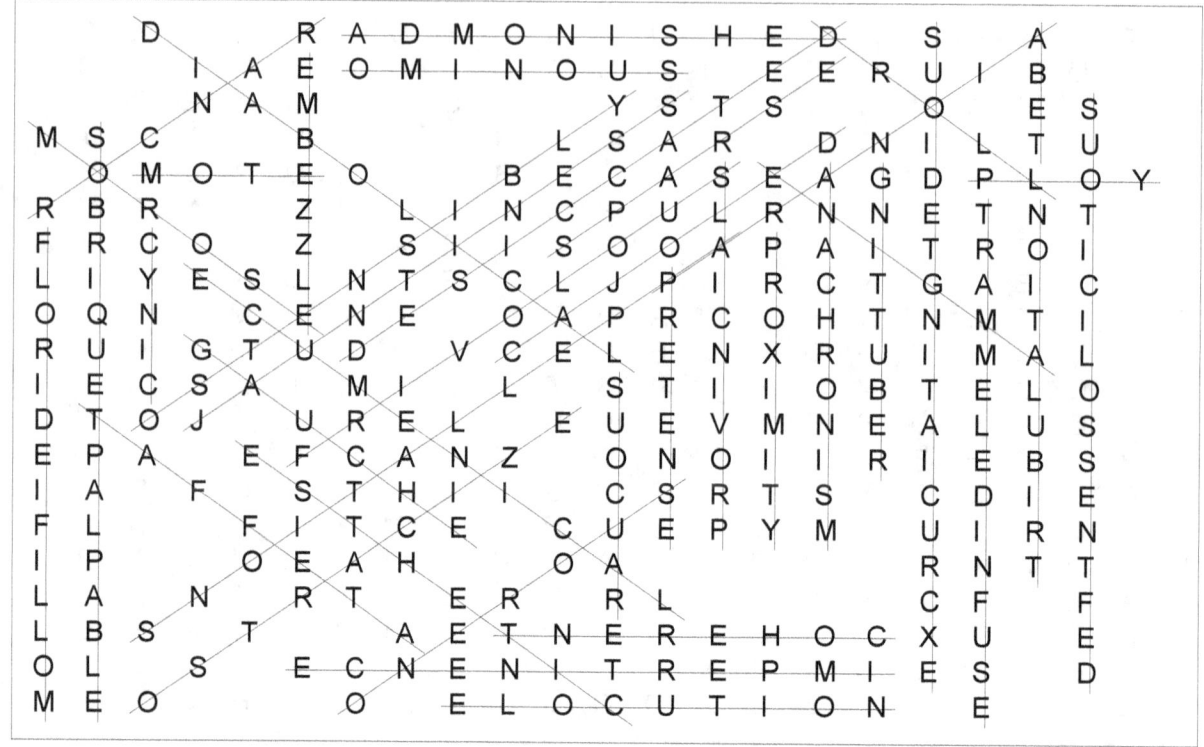

A crisp fabric with a slight sheen (7)
A speck (4)
Amusingly odd (5)
An action done to frustrate (4)
An affectionate nickname (9)
Appearing as such (10)
Appreciating beauty (8)
Bitter, long-lasting resentment (6)
Boldness (12)
Calmed, soothed (9)
Capable of being touched or felt (8)
Characteristic of the devil (10)
Closeness (9)
Dried out, arid (10)
Expressing care or concern (10)
Extreme, irrational distrust of others (8)
False appearance (8)
Gently reproved (10)
Gloomy (6)
Having a buoyant or self-confident air (10)
Intensely painful (12)
Lacking social polish; tactless (6)
Menacing; threatening (7)
Names, titles, or designations (12)

Occurring at widely spaced intervals (6)
One who believes others are selfish (5)
Out of proper or chronological order (11)
Promoting unity among religions (10)
Public speaking (9)
Refuting (9)
Restricted, restrained (9)
Rosy colored (6)
Rough-sounding (7)
Silly (9)
Something puzzling or inexplicable (6)
Sticking together (8)
Suffering (11)
Tiresome due to extreme slowness (7)
To encourage or help (4)
To exclude from a group (9)
To fill with something (6)
To take money or property and violate a trust (8)
Troublesome (7)
Unsophisticated people (11)
Urged gently (7)
Quickness; skillfulness (8)

Caged Bird Vocabulary Word Search 3

```
M N V C P Q E Z I C A R T S O F B R D H N R S G T
N X Y S U O N I M O D E L O J A C E A S C K A R S
K H E H L S F P R F R D Q Z Q X L U N A U I S T
S T S I H C O S A M E L O C U T I O N S C B U U W
D E R N V Q Y P S P A B O L E A I N B H U O E O D
E S A B N B H N S C E C U R L T N X E L C U R T T
F I P T K O P N I M H R O T I B Y D A U T R A I J
T A S H R L E L V C O U T D T D K T A E R G P C S
N L Q I B O O S I F S R E U E I I R T R B E P I H
E A S H D B U N T F Q P O B R O N A E M Y O R L J
S M X B A E F B Y H X C U S N E R G F O Z I O O Z
S F W I P T S B A E E T R S E U S N F T M S B S T
Z H D H R A O I R D A T U F S C U I A E O I A U Q
P V P W O P B Q C N O O I N N O O D T G L E T O W
L L Y K X I R R T C R U E C E H L U H K L E I I L
S F O V I S I E S E A M R K T E O A D R I N O D R
M P W Y M S Q Y N W M T R S E R V R J B F I N E B
N L B F I I U O D O Y B E S R E I A S U I G R T X
Q H K X T D E C C H V Q M D P N R M S V E M Q V L
T Z Y S Y B T P A L P A B L E T F E W B D A J R G
```

ABET
APERTURES
APHORISMS
APPROBATION
BOURGEOISIE
CAJOLED
COHERENT
COMMENSURATE
CYNIC
DEBUTANTE
DEFTNESS
DESICCATED
DEXTEROUS
DIABOLICAL
DISSIPATE
DROLL
ELOCUTION

ENIGMA
ESTHETIC
EXPEDITIOUS
FLORID
FRIVOLOUS
GAUCHE
IMPASSIVITY
INFUSE
MALAISE
MARAUDING
MASOCHISTS
MOLLIFIED
MOROSE
MOTE
OMINOUS
ONEROUS
OSTRACIZE

PALPABLE
PLOY
PRETENSE
PROXIMITY
QUANDARY
RANCOR
RAUCOUS
REBUTTING
SOBRIQUET
SOLICITOUS
SPARSE
TAFFETA
TEDIOUS
TRIBULATION
TROUBADOURS

Caged Bird Vocabulary Word Search 3 Answer Key

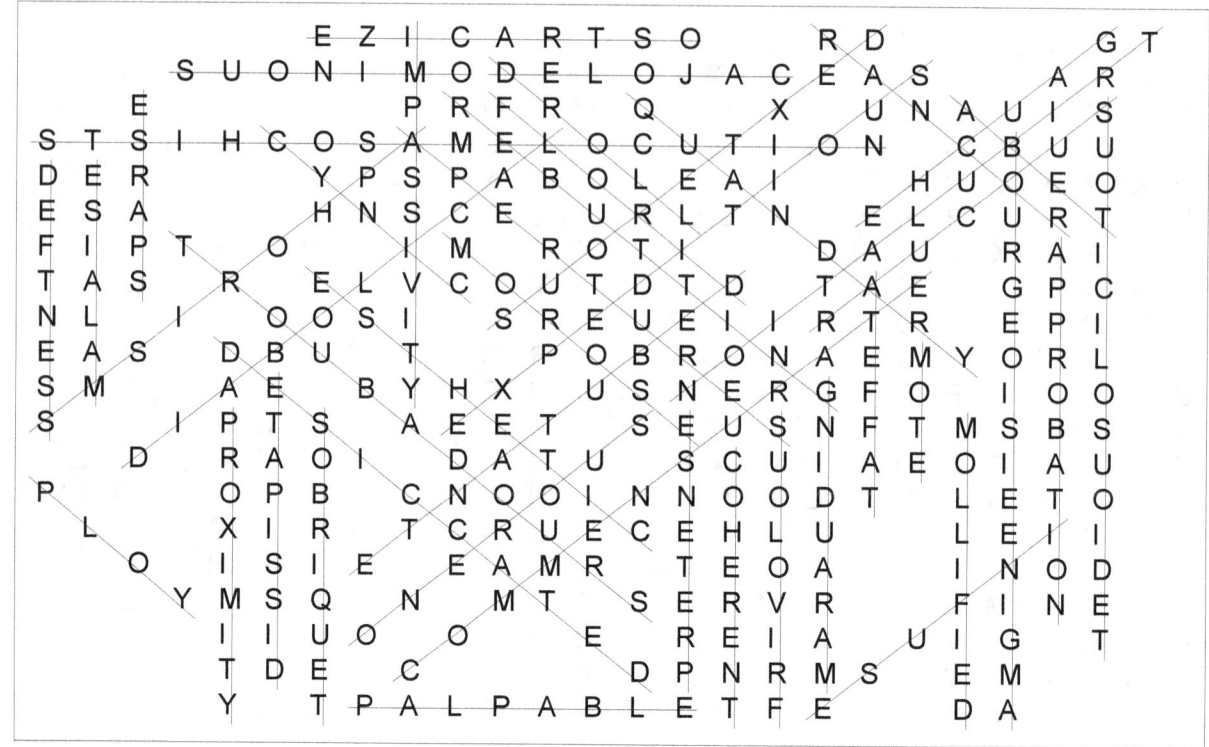

ABET	ENIGMA	PALPABLE
APERTURES	ESTHETIC	PLOY
APHORISMS	EXPEDITIOUS	PRETENSE
APPROBATION	FLORID	PROXIMITY
BOURGEOISIE	FRIVOLOUS	QUANDARY
CAJOLED	GAUCHE	RANCOR
COHERENT	IMPASSIVITY	RAUCOUS
COMMENSURATE	INFUSE	REBUTTING
CYNIC	MALAISE	SOBRIQUET
DEBUTANTE	MARAUDING	SOLICITOUS
DEFTNESS	MASOCHISTS	SPARSE
DESICCATED	MOLLIFIED	TAFFETA
DEXTEROUS	MOROSE	TEDIOUS
DIABOLICAL	MOTE	TRIBULATION
DISSIPATE	OMINOUS	TROUBADOURS
DROLL	ONEROUS	
ELOCUTION	OSTRACIZE	

Caged Bird Vocabulary Word Search 4

```
W E L O C U T I O N D L S S R U O D A B U O R T J
K F P S E L Z Z E B M E U V A P P R O B A T I O N
T R D T H J D N C X T O F L C A C O P H O N Y I A
R I A E C U M E N I C A L E S I A L A M Y R N M D
A V T N F Z G P X U Y R F V R D X L H O A C G P E
M O E S F T S M A T L C U T D E P C L B I I E A B
M L F I G L N R R L E A H C N C N P E N N S P S U
E O F B B B A E T G P R C Q I G F T Y E U E A S T
L U A L F O B M S E R A O E A A T C I F T D R I A
E S T Y P U Y L B S D C B U R M T M N A M L A V N
D M G A T R N T Q O Z I C L S A G I P O L V N I T
N X O T P G A O M D Y H O I E M T I N D P S O T E
T F I L X E E P S A E A N U M Q S I N G U U I Y L
S N L Q L O R S H T R O N K S S S Q O O M O A R Z
G P K O J I T T T O R A Z T I H V R R N O N V A Z
C W A M R S F D U H R A U D E P G E T C R I N N C
B W D R S I V I C R E I C D P B N R K L O M N C J
G F D L S E D A E X E T S I I O F X N D S O B O T
C O H E R E N T H D D S I M Z N K E S N E T E R P
Y S D E T A R T E P R E P C S E G Q U A N D A R Y
```

ABET
ADMONISHED
ANACHRONISM
APERTURES
APHORISMS
APPROBATION
BOURGEOISIE
CACOPHONY
COHERENT
CYNIC
DEBUTANTE
DEFERENTIAL
DEFTNESS
DEXTEROUS
DISSIPATE
DROLL
ECUMENICAL
ELOCUTION
EMBEZZLE
ENIGMA
ESTHETIC
EXCRUCIATING
FLAMBOYANT
FLORID
FRIVOLOUS
GAUCHE
IMPASSIVITY
INFUSE
LACERATION
MALAISE
MARAUDING
MOLLIFIED
MOROSE
MOTE
OMINOUS
ONEROUS
OSTENSIBLY
OSTRACIZE
PALPABLE
PARANOIA
PERPETRATED
PLOY
PRETENSE
QUANDARY
RANCOR
RAUCOUS
REBUTTING
SPARSE
TAFFETA
TEDIOUS
TRAMMELED
TROUBADOURS

Caged Bird Vocabulary Word Search 4 Answer Key

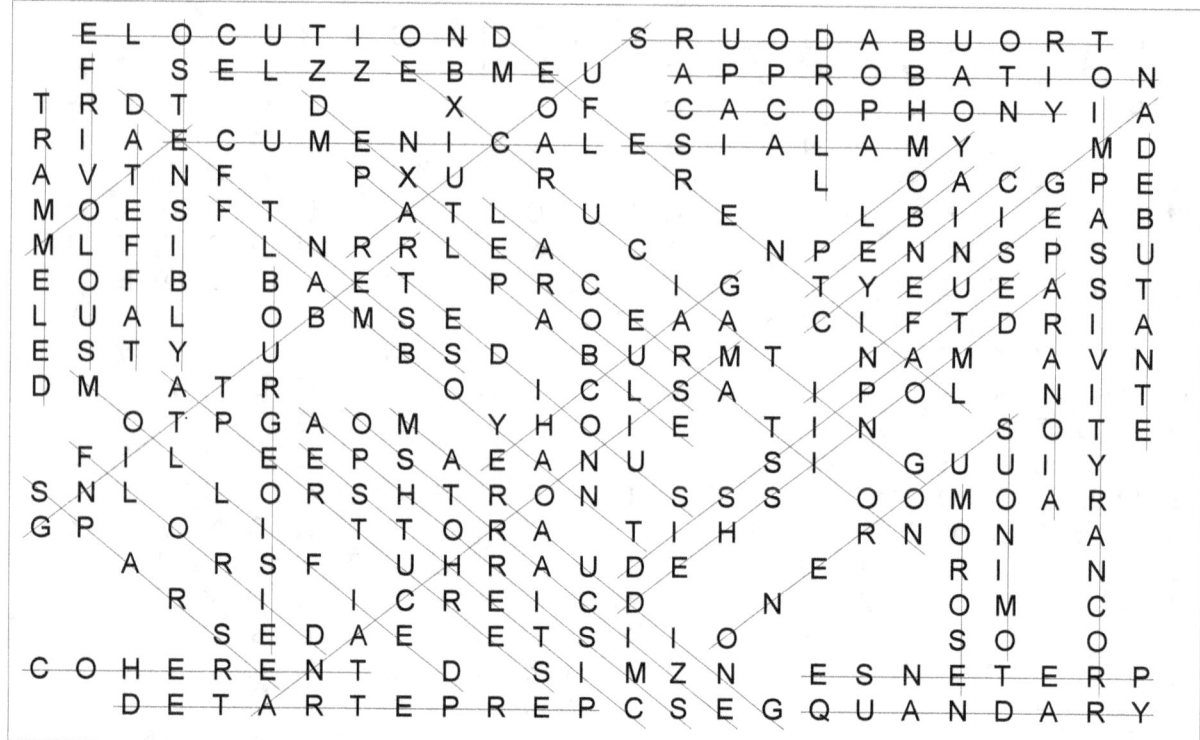

ABET	EMBEZZLE	OSTENSIBLY
ADMONISHED	ENIGMA	OSTRACIZE
ANACHRONISM	ESTHETIC	PALPABLE
APERTURES	EXCRUCIATING	PARANOIA
APHORISMS	FLAMBOYANT	PERPETRATED
APPROBATION	FLORID	PLOY
BOURGEOISIE	FRIVOLOUS	PRETENSE
CACOPHONY	GAUCHE	QUANDARY
COHERENT	IMPASSIVITY	RANCOR
CYNIC	INFUSE	RAUCOUS
DEBUTANTE	LACERATION	REBUTTING
DEFERENTIAL	MALAISE	SPARSE
DEFTNESS	MARAUDING	TAFFETA
DEXTEROUS	MOLLIFIED	TEDIOUS
DISSIPATE	MOROSE	TRAMMELED
DROLL	MOTE	TROUBADOURS
ECUMENICAL	OMINOUS	
ELOCUTION	ONEROUS	

Caged Bird Vocabulary Crossword 1

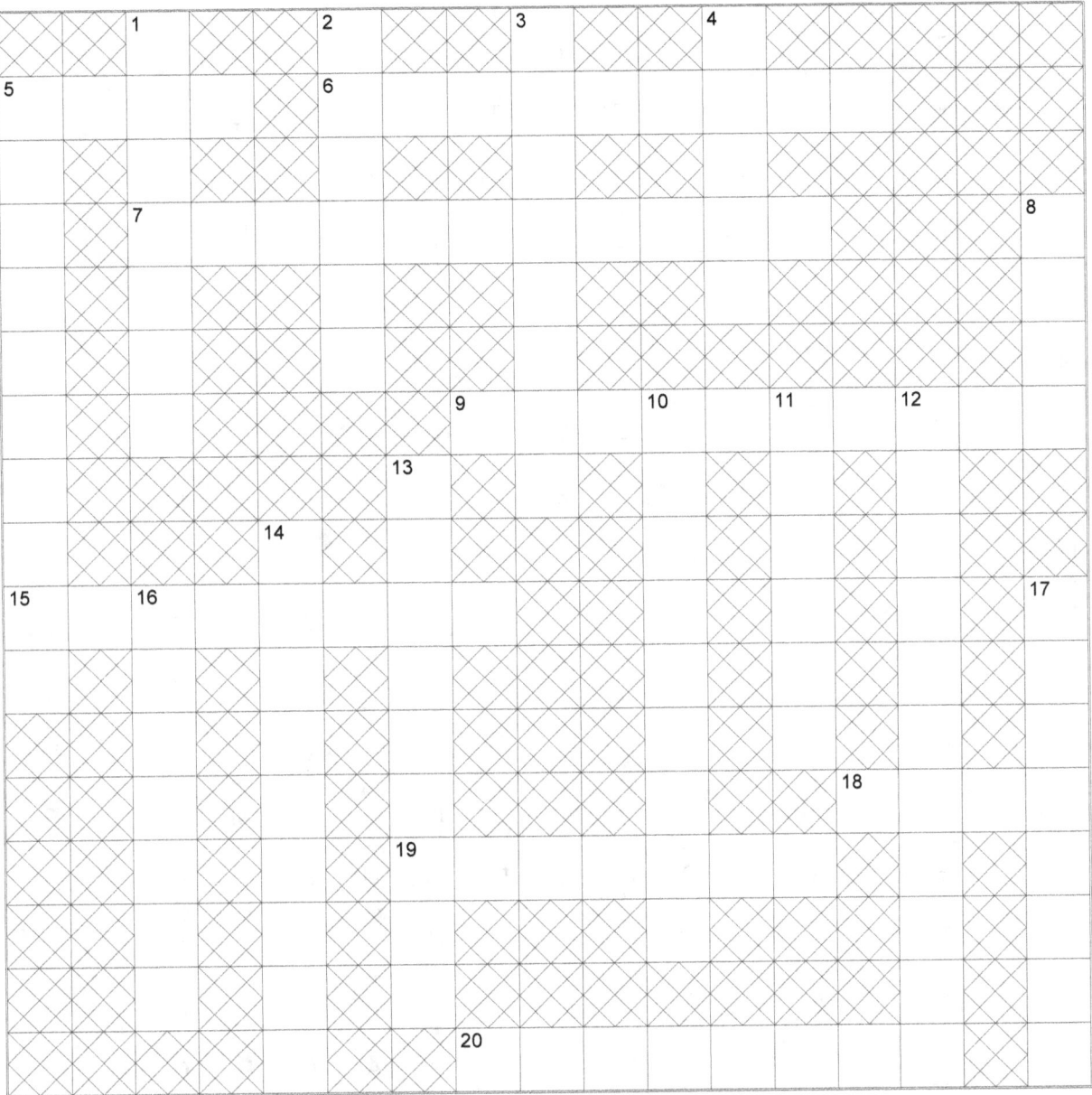

Across
5. To encourage or help
6. Openings
7. Difficult to understand
9. Appearing as such
15. Appreciating beauty
18. A speck
19. Troublesome
20. Capable of being touched or felt

Down
1. Tiresome due to extreme slowness
2. Lacking social polish; tactless
3. False appearance
4. Amusingly odd
5. Gently reproved
8. An action done to frustrate
10. Public speaking
11. Occurring at widely spaced intervals
12. The middle class
13. Silly
14. A young woman entering society
16. A crisp fabric with a slight sheen
17. Sticking together

Caged Bird Vocabulary Crossword 1 Answer Key

		1 T		2 G			3 P			4 D			
5 A	B	E	T	6 A	P	E	R	T	U	R	E	S	
D		D		U			E			O			
M		7 I	N	S	C	R	U	T	A	B	L	E	8 P
O		O		H			E			L			L
N		U		E			N						O
I		S				9 O	S	10 T	E	11 N	S	12 I	B	L	Y
S				13 F	E		L		P		O	
H			14 D	R			O		A		U	
15 E	16 S	T	H	E	T	I	C		C		R		R	17 C
D		A		B	U		V		O		U		S		G	O
		F		U			O		T		E		E		H
		F		T			L		I			18 M	O	T	E
		E		A		19 O	N	E	R	O	U	S		I		R
		T		N		U			N			S		E
		A		T		S						I		N
				E		20 P	A	L	P	A	B	L	E		T

Across
5. To encourage or help
6. Openings
7. Difficult to understand
9. Appearing as such
15. Appreciating beauty
18. A speck
19. Troublesome
20. Capable of being touched or felt

Down
1. Tiresome due to extreme slowness
2. Lacking social polish; tactless
3. False appearance
4. Amusingly odd
5. Gently reproved
8. An action done to frustrate
10. Public speaking
11. Occurring at widely spaced intervals
12. The middle class
13. Silly
14. A young woman entering society
16. A crisp fabric with a slight sheen
17. Sticking together

Caged Bird Vocabulary Crossword 2

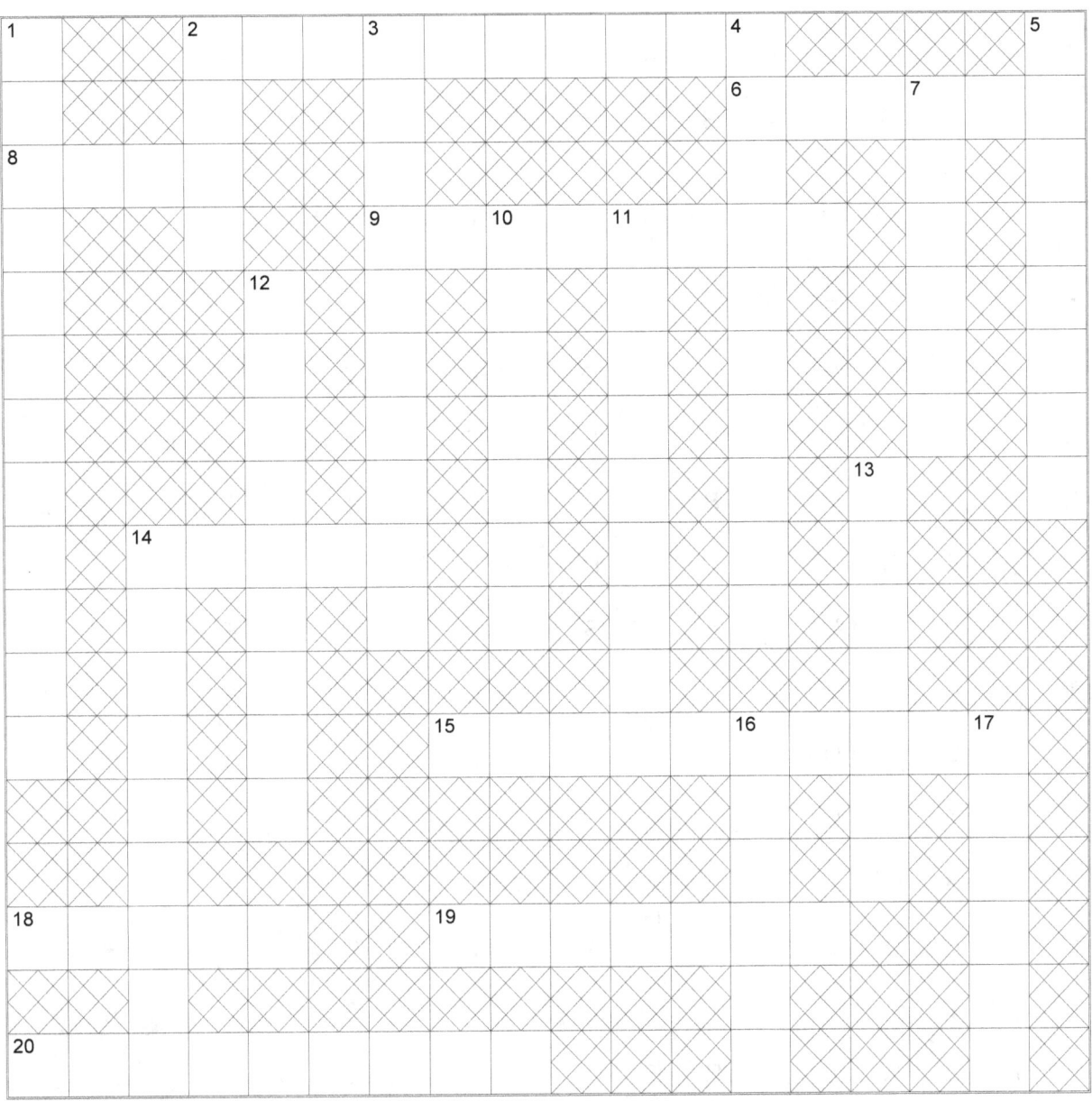

Across
2. Gently reproved
6. Something puzzling or inexplicable
8. A speck
9. Appreciating beauty
14. Amusingly odd
15. Having a buoyant or self-confident air
18. One who believes others are selfish
19. Rough-sounding
20. Openings

Down
1. Of the same size or proportion
2. To encourage or help
3. Appearing as such
4. Dried out, arid
5. Capable of being touched or felt
7. Lacking social polish; tactless
10. Tiresome due to extreme slowness
11. Public speaking
12. Silly
13. A crisp fabric with a slight sheen
14. A young woman entering society
16. To fill with something
17. Occurring at widely spaced intervals

Caged Bird Vocabulary Crossword 2 Answer Key

¹C		²A	D	³M	O	N	I	S	H	⁴E	D		⁵P
O		B		S						⁶E	N	I	⁷G	M	A
⁸M	O	T	E							S			A		L
M		T		⁹E	S	¹⁰T	H	¹¹E	T	I	C		U		P
E			¹²F	N		E		L		C			C		A
N			R	S		D		O		C			H		B
S			I	I		I		C		A			E		L
U			V	B		O		U		T		¹³T			E
R		¹⁴D	R	O	L	L		U		T		E		A	
A		E		L		Y		S		I		D		F	
T		B		O						O				F	
E		U		U			¹⁵J	A	U	N	¹⁶T	I	N	E	S	¹⁷S
		T		S							N				T		P
		A									F				A		A
¹⁸C	Y	N	I	C		¹⁹R	A	U	C	O	U	S			R
		T									S				S
²⁰A	P	E	R	T	U	R	E	S			E				E

Across
2. Gently reproved
6. Something puzzling or inexplicable
8. A speck
9. Appreciating beauty
14. Amusingly odd
15. Having a buoyant or self-confident air
18. One who believes others are selfish
19. Rough-sounding
20. Openings

Down
1. Of the same size or proportion
2. To encourage or help
3. Appearing as such
4. Dried out, arid
5. Capable of being touched or felt
7. Lacking social polish; tactless
10. Tiresome due to extreme slowness
11. Public speaking
12. Silly
13. A crisp fabric with a slight sheen
14. A young woman entering society
16. To fill with something
17. Occurring at widely spaced intervals

Caged Bird Vocabulary Crossword 3

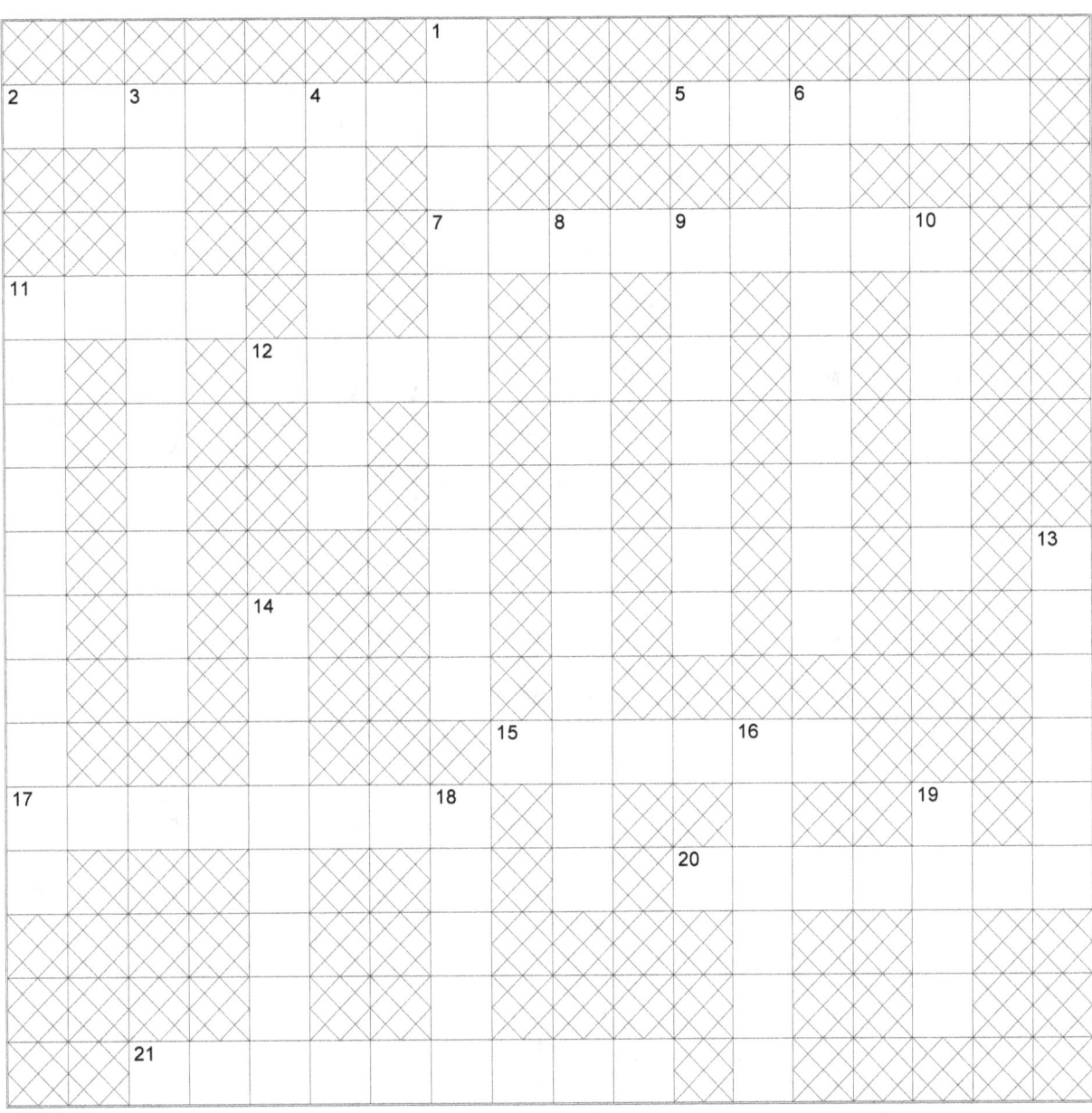

Across
2. Public speaking
5. To fill with something
7. Refuting
11. To encourage or help
12. A speck
15. Gloomy
17. Appreciating beauty
20. Urged gently
21. To exclude from a group

Down
1. The middle class
3. Appearing as such
4. Tiresome due to extreme slowness
6. Silly
8. Speaking irreverently of a sacred entity
9. A crisp fabric with a slight sheen
10. Lacking social polish; tactless
11. Gently reproved
13. Rosy colored
14. Sticking together
16. Occurring at widely spaced intervals
18. One who believes others are selfish
19. An action done to frustrate

Caged Bird Vocabulary Crossword 3 Answer Key

							1 B					
2 E	L	3 O	C	4 U	T	I	O	N		5 I	N	6 F	U	S	E

(Across)
- 2. Public speaking — ELOCUTION
- 3. Appearing as such — OSTENSIBLY
- 4. Tiresome due to extreme slowness — TEDIOUS
- 5. To fill with something — INFUSE
- 6. Silly — FRIVOLOUS
- 7. Refuting — REBUTTING
- 8. Speaking irreverently of a sacred entity — BLASPHEMES
- 9. A crisp fabric with a slight sheen — TAFFETA
- 10. Lacking social polish; tactless — GAUCHE
- 11. To encourage or help — ABET
- 11. Gently reproved — ADMONISHED
- 12. A speck — MOTE
- 13. Rosy colored — FLORID... (FLO...)
- 14. Sticking together — COHERENT
- 15. Gloomy — MOROSE
- 16. Occurring at widely spaced intervals — SPORADIC... (SEP...)
- 17. Appreciating beauty — ESTHETIC
- 18. One who believes others are selfish — CYNIC... (CYNI...)
- 19. An action done to frustrate — PLOY
- 20. Urged gently — CAJOLED
- 21. To exclude from a group — OSTRACIZE

Down
 1. The middle class — BOURGEOISIE

Across
 2. Public speaking
 5. To fill with something
 7. Refuting
11. To encourage or help
12. A speck
15. Gloomy
17. Appreciating beauty
20. Urged gently
21. To exclude from a group

Down
 1. The middle class

 3. Appearing as such
 4. Tiresome due to extreme slowness
 6. Silly
 8. Speaking irreverently of a sacred entity
 9. A crisp fabric with a slight sheen
10. Lacking social polish; tactless
11. Gently reproved
13. Rosy colored
14. Sticking together
16. Occurring at widely spaced intervals
18. One who believes others are selfish
19. An action done to frustrate

Caged Bird Vocabulary Crossword 4

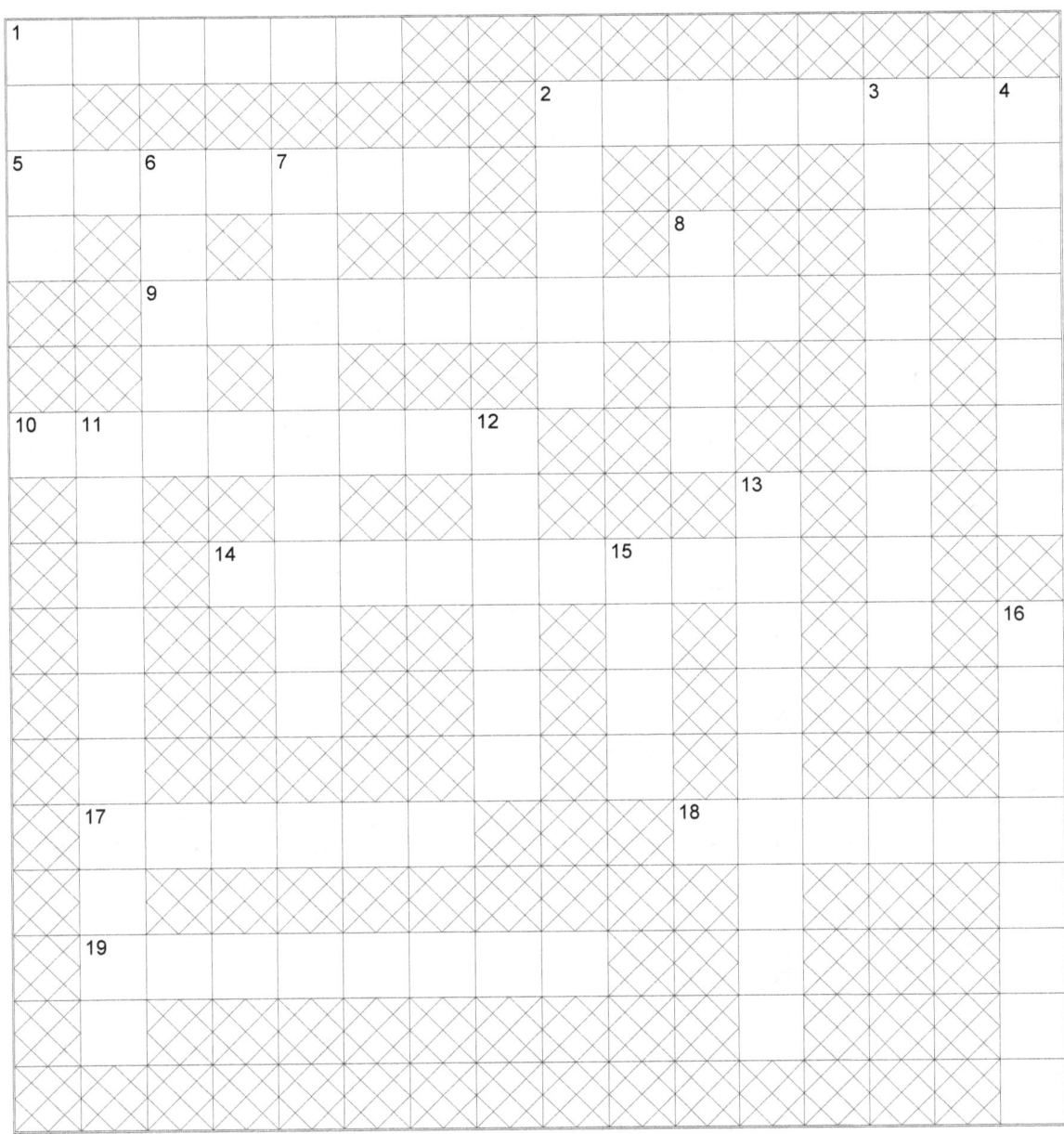

Across
1. Gloomy
2. Sticking together
5. Tiresome due to extreme slowness
9. Appearing as such
10. Capable of being touched or felt
14. To drive away; disperse
17. Occurring at widely spaced intervals
18. Lacking social polish; tactless
19. Appreciating beauty

Down
1. A speck
2. One who believes others are selfish
3. Public speaking
4. A crisp fabric with a slight sheen
6. Amusingly odd
7. To exclude from a group
8. An action done to frustrate
11. Gently reproved
12. Something puzzling or inexplicable
13. A young woman entering society
15. To encourage or help
16. To take money or property and violate a trust

Caged Bird Vocabulary Crossword 4 Answer Key

¹M	O	R	O	S	E					
O					²C	O	H	E	³R	E	⁴N	T
⁵T	⁶E	I	⁷O	U	S		Y			L		A
E	R		S				N	⁸P		O		F
	⁹O	S	T	E	N	S	I	B	L	Y	C	F
	L		R				C		O		U	E
¹⁰P	¹¹A	L	P	A	B	L	E	¹²E		Y		T		A
	D			C				N		¹³D		I	T	A
	M		¹⁴D	I	S	S	I	P	¹⁵A	T	E		O	
	O		Z					G	B		B	N		¹⁶E
	N		E					M	E		T			M
	I							A	T		T			B
	¹⁷S	P	A	R	S	E			¹⁸G	A	U	C	H	E
	H								N					Z
	¹⁹E	S	T	H	E	T	I	C		T				Z
	D									E				L
														E

Across
1. Gloomy
2. Sticking together
5. Tiresome due to extreme slowness
9. Appearing as such
10. Capable of being touched or felt
14. To drive away; disperse
17. Occurring at widely spaced intervals
18. Lacking social polish; tactless
19. Appreciating beauty

Down
1. A speck
2. One who believes others are selfish
3. Public speaking
4. A crisp fabric with a slight sheen
6. Amusingly odd
7. To exclude from a group
8. An action done to frustrate
11. Gently reproved
12. Something puzzling or inexplicable
13. A young woman entering society
15. To encourage or help
16. To take money or property and violate a trust

Caged Bird Vocabulary Juggle Letters 1

1. SEDDHANIOM = 1. _____
   Gently reproved

2. ETBA = 2. _____
   To encourage or help

3. IGENAM = 3. _____
   Something puzzling or inexplicable

4. NNIOTCARMERIIS = 4. _____
   Countercharges

5. EMADLMTRE = 5. _____
   Restricted, restrained

6. UCCATXEIIGNR = 6. _____
   Intensely painful

7. PPOAIBRTNOA = 7. _____
   An expression of warm approval; praise

8. ETRESPNE = 8. _____
   False appearance

9. NEAUBDTTE = 9. _____
   A young woman entering society

10. SEDEFTSN = 10. _____
    Quickness; skillfulness

11. MOORSE = 11. _____
    Gloomy

12. TSLNIEBYOS = 12. _____
    Appearing as such

13. EUSTNJASIN = 13. _____
    Having a buoyant or self-confident air

14. RAAYNQUD = 14. _____
    A state of uncertainty or perplexity

15. UROCASU = 15. _____
    Rough-sounding

Caged Bird Vocabulary Juggle Letters 1 Answer Key

1. SEDDHANIOM = 1. ADMONISHED
   Gently reproved

2. ETBA = 2. ABET
   To encourage or help

3. IGENAM = 3. ENIGMA
   Something puzzling or inexplicable

4. NNIOTCARMERIIS = 4. RECRIMINATIONS
   Countercharges

5. EMADLMTRE = 5. TRAMMELED
   Restricted, restrained

6. UCCATXEIIGNR = 6. EXCRUCIATING
   Intensely painful

7. PPOAIBRTNOA = 7. APPROBATION
   An expression of warm approval; praise

8. ETRESPNE = 8. PRETENSE
   False appearance

9. NEAUBDTTE = 9. DEBUTANTE
   A young woman entering society

10. SEDEFTSN =10. DEFTNESS
    Quickness; skillfulness

11. MOORSE =11. MOROSE
    Gloomy

12. TSLNIEBYOS =12. OSTENSIBLY
    Appearing as such

13. EUSTNJASIN =13. JAUNTINESS
    Having a buoyant or self-confident air

14. RAAYNQUD =14. QUANDARY
    A state of uncertainty or perplexity

15. UROCASU =15. RAUCOUS
    Rough-sounding

Caged Bird Vocabulary Juggle Letters 2

1. VPSOICRILAN = 1. _____
   Unsophisticated people

2. AEALSMI = 2. _____
   A general sense of depression

3. PTAIBNRPOOA = 3. _____
   An expression of warm approval; praise

4. OAAPNAIR = 4. _____
   Extreme, irrational distrust of others

5. AIDALCBIOL = 5. _____
   Characteristic of the devil

6. TNACNONALH = 6. _____
   Coolly unconcerned or indifferent

7. AIMNGE = 7. _____
   Something puzzling or inexplicable

8. SEUARETRP = 8. _____
   Openings

9. NERISOICTRIMNA = 9. _____
   Countercharges

10. BEAT = 10. _____
    To encourage or help

11. BPEALAPL = 11. _____
    Capable of being touched or felt

12. RTBREEUVITI = 12. _____
    Demanded in repayment

13. TFNLOAAYMB = 13. _____
    Highly elaborate, showy

14. EEDTARNFLEI = 14. _____
    Courteous, respectful

15. RLDFIO = 15. _____
    Rosy colored

Caged Bird Vocabulary Juggle Letters 2 Answer Key

1. VPSOICRILAN = 1. PROVINCIALS
   Unsophisticated people

2. AEALSMI = 2. MALAISE
   A general sense of depression

3. PTAIBNRPOOA = 3. APPROBATION
   An expression of warm approval; praise

4. OAAPNAIR = 4. PARANOIA
   Extreme, irrational distrust of others

5. AIDALCBIOL = 5. DIABOLICAL
   Characteristic of the devil

6. TNACNONALH = 6. NONCHALANT
   Coolly unconcerned or indifferent

7. AIMNGE = 7. ENIGMA
   Something puzzling or inexplicable

8. SEUARETRP = 8. APERTURES
   Openings

9. NERISOICTRIMNA = 9. RECRIMINATIONS
   Countercharges

10. BEAT =10. ABET
    To encourage or help

11. BPEALAPL =11. PALPABLE
    Capable of being touched or felt

12. RTBREEUVITI =12. RETRIBUTIVE
    Demanded in repayment

13. TFNLOAAYMB =13. FLAMBOYANT
    Highly elaborate, showy

14. EEDTARNFLEI =14. DEFERENTIAL
    Courteous, respectful

15. RLDFIO =15. FLORID
    Rosy colored

Caged Bird Vocabulary Juggle Letters 3

1. AEGINM = 1. _____
Something puzzling or inexplicable

2. ZLBMEZEE = 2. _____
To take money or property and violate a trust

3. AUCEIMECNL = 3. _____
Promoting unity among religions

4. INATCRIUCGXE = 4. _____
Intensely painful

5. UOERSNO = 5. _____
Troublesome

6. ETORNHEC = 6. _____
Sticking together

7. EUSHSALOPMB = 7. _____
Speaking irreverently of a sacred entity

8. IYCCN = 8. _____
One who believes others are selfish

9. NNEIMPDMAUO = 9. _____
Wild uproar or noise

10. TEAB =10. _____
To encourage or help

11. NIORAAAP =11. _____
Extreme, irrational distrust of others

12. SVOIORFLU =12. _____
Silly

13. IPROIYMXT =13. _____
Closeness

14. IHEETTSC =14. _____
Appreciating beauty

15. IYTLOESBNS =15. _____
Appearing as such

Caged Bird Vocabulary Juggle Letters 3 Answer Key

1. AEGINM = 1. ENIGMA
Something puzzling or inexplicable

2. ZLBMEZEE = 2. EMBEZZLE
To take money or property and violate a trust

3. AUCEIMECNL = 3. ECUMENICAL
Promoting unity among religions

4. INATCRIUCGXE = 4. EXCRUCIATING
Intensely painful

5. UOERSNO = 5. ONEROUS
Troublesome

6. ETORNHEC = 6. COHERENT
Sticking together

7. EUSHSALOPMB = 7. BLASPHEMOUS
Speaking irreverently of a sacred entity

8. IYCCN = 8. CYNIC
One who believes others are selfish

9. NNEIMPDMAUO = 9. PANDEMONIUM
Wild uproar or noise

10. TEAB = 10. ABET
To encourage or help

11. NIORAAAP = 11. PARANOIA
Extreme, irrational distrust of others

12. SVOIORFLU = 12. FRIVOLOUS
Silly

13. IPROIYMXT = 13. PROXIMITY
Closeness

14. IHEETTSC = 14. ESTHETIC
Appreciating beauty

15. IYTLOESBNS = 15. OSTENSIBLY
Appearing as such

Caged Bird Vocabulary Juggle Letters 4

1. SOCIMAARHNN = 1. _____
   Out of proper or chronological order

2. EUOGBIOIESR = 2. _____
   The middle class

3. APLAPEBL = 3. _____
   Capable of being touched or felt

4. UCEGHA = 4. _____
   Lacking social polish; tactless

5. TATEAFF = 5. _____
   A crisp fabric with a slight sheen

6. AJLCDOE = 6. _____
   Urged gently

7. ANRILTOCAE = 7. _____
   A jagged, deep cut

8. RARTUSPEE = 8. _____
   Openings

9. DARMLEMTE = 9. _____
   Restricted, restrained

10. ANIRAAOP = 10. _____
    Extreme, irrational distrust of others

11. INEPMTNCERIE = 11. _____
    Boldness

12. TOOEUCLNI = 12. _____
    Public speaking

13. TEBA = 13. _____
    To encourage or help

14. HTOSSASICM = 14. _____
    Those who get pleasure from being mistreated

15. ORTBTILUNAI = 15. _____
    Suffering

Caged Bird Vocabulary Juggle Letters 4 Answer Key

1. SOCIMAARHNN = 1. ANACHRONISM
   Out of proper or chronological order

2. EUOGBIOIESR = 2. BOURGEOISIE
   The middle class

3. APLAPEBL = 3. PALPABLE
   Capable of being touched or felt

4. UCEGHA = 4. GAUCHE
   Lacking social polish; tactless

5. TATEAFF = 5. TAFFETA
   A crisp fabric with a slight sheen

6. AJLCDOE = 6. CAJOLED
   Urged gently

7. ANRILTOCAE = 7. LACERATION
   A jagged, deep cut

8. RARTUSPEE = 8. APERTURES
   Openings

9. DARMLEMTE = 9. TRAMMELED
   Restricted, restrained

10. ANIRAAOP = 10. PARANOIA
    Extreme, irrational distrust of others

11. INEPMTNCERIE = 11. IMPERTINENCE
    Boldness

12. TOOEUCLNI = 12. ELOCUTION
    Public speaking

13. TEBA = 13. ABET
    To encourage or help

14. HTOSSASICM = 14. MASOCHISTS
    Those who get pleasure from being mistreated

15. ORTBTILUNAI = 15. TRIBULATION
    Suffering

ABET	To encourage or help
ADMONISHED	Gently reproved
ANACHRONISM	Out of proper or chronological order
APERTURES	Openings
APHORISMS	Brief statements of principles
APPELLATIONS	Names, titles, or designations

APPROBATION	An expression of warm approval; praise
BLASPHEMOUS	Speaking irreverently of a sacred entity
BOURGEOISIE	The middle class
CACOPHONY	Jarring, discordant sound
CAJOLED	Urged gently
CAPRICIOUSNESS	Impulsiveness

COHERENT	Sticking together
COMMENSURATE	Of the same size or proportion
CONDESCENSION	Acting in a patronizingly superior way
CYNIC	One who believes others are selfish
DEBUTANTE	A young woman entering society
DEFERENTIAL	Courteous, respectful

DEFTNESS	Quickness; skillfulness
DESICCATED	Dried out, arid
DEXTEROUS	Mentally skillful
DIABOLICAL	Characteristic of the devil
DISSIPATE	To drive away; disperse
DROLL	Amusingly odd

ECUMENICAL	Promoting unity among religions
ELOCUTION	Public speaking
EMBEZZLE	To take money or property and violate a trust
ENIGMA	Something puzzling or inexplicable
ESTHETIC	Appreciating beauty
EXCRUCIATING	Intensely painful

EXPEDITIOUS	Done with speed and efficiency
FLAMBOYANT	Highly elaborate, showy
FLORID	Rosy colored
FRIVOLOUS	Silly
GAUCHE	Lacking social polish; tactless
IMPASSIVITY	Revealing no emotion

IMPERTINENCE	Boldness
INFUSE	To fill with something
INSCRUTABLE	Difficult to understand
JAUNTINESS	Having a buoyant or self-confident air
LACERATION	A jagged, deep cut
MALAISE	A general sense of depression

MARAUDING	Raiding to plunder
MASOCHISTS	Those who get pleasure from being mistreated
MOLLIFIED	Calmed, soothed
MOROSE	Gloomy
MOTE	A speck
NONCHALANT	Coolly unconcerned or indifferent

OMINOUS	Menacing; threatening
ONEROUS	Troublesome
OSTENSIBLY	Appearing as such
OSTRACIZE	To exclude from a group
PALPABLE	Capable of being touched or felt
PANDEMONIUM	Wild uproar or noise

PARANOIA	Extreme, irrational distrust of others
PERPETRATED	Committed
PLOY	An action done to frustrate
PRETENSE	False appearance
PROVINCIALS	Unsophisticated people
PROXIMITY	Closeness

QUANDARY	A state of uncertainty or perplexity
RANCOR	Bitter, long-lasting resentment
RAUCOUS	Rough-sounding
REBUTTING	Refuting
RECRIMINATIONS	Countercharges
RETRIBUTIVE	Demanded in repayment

SOBRIQUET	An affectionate nickname
SOLICITOUS	Expressing care or concern
SPARSE	Occurring at widely spaced intervals
SUPERCILIOUS	Showing haughty disdain
TAFFETA	A crisp fabric with a slight sheen
TEDIOUS	Tiresome due to extreme slowness

TRAMMELED	Restricted, restrained
TRIBULATION	Suffering
TROUBADOURS	Strolling minstrels

Caged Bird Vocabulary

APPELLATIONS	IMPASSIVITY	MOLLIFIED	JAUNTINESS	BOURGEOISIE
PERPETRATED	ABET	FRIVOLOUS	RANCOR	PROVINCIALS
EXPEDITIOUS	DEBUTANTE	FREE SPACE	MASOCHISTS	DEFTNESS
DISSIPATE	INSCRUTABLE	PRETENSE	ANACHRONISM	TRAMMELED
INFUSE	BLASPHEMOUS	APERTURES	OSTRACIZE	DROLL

Caged Bird Vocabulary

LACERATION	APHORISMS	SPARSE	ESTHETIC	RAUCOUS
CYNIC	ADMONISHED	SUPERCILIOUS	FLORID	NONCHALANT
ECUMENICAL	IMPERTINENCE	FREE SPACE	MARAUDING	TROUBADOURS
APPROBATION	GAUCHE	TEDIOUS	RECRIMINATIONS	ONEROUS
PARANOIA	COMMENSURATE	EMBEZZLE	DEXTEROUS	RETRIBUTIVE

Caged Bird Vocabulary

OMINOUS	APPELLATIONS	BLASPHEMOUS	RANCOR	APERTURES
CAJOLED	PALPABLE	ONEROUS	PERPETRATED	RECRIMINATIONS
APHORISMS	PLOY	FREE SPACE	TRIBULATION	APPROBATION
RAUCOUS	SUPERCILIOUS	TEDIOUS	ELOCUTION	DISSIPATE
LACERATION	PANDEMONIUM	FLORID	DESICCATED	DEXTEROUS

Caged Bird Vocabulary

CONDESCENSION	PARANOIA	PROXIMITY	JAUNTINESS	RETRIBUTIVE
SPARSE	MOROSE	PROVINCIALS	QUANDARY	OSTRACIZE
INSCRUTABLE	PRETENSE	FREE SPACE	COHERENT	ADMONISHED
MOLLIFIED	FRIVOLOUS	MARAUDING	COMMENSURATE	INFUSE
DEFTNESS	DROLL	CACOPHONY	IMPERTINENCE	MOTE

Caged Bird Vocabulary

TAFFETA	PERPETRATED	DEFERENTIAL	CAJOLED	PARANOIA
TROUBADOURS	PROXIMITY	ESTHETIC	PRETENSE	APHORISMS
NONCHALANT	MOTE	FREE SPACE	MARAUDING	APPELLATIONS
DISSIPATE	ECUMENICAL	INSCRUTABLE	ADMONISHED	REBUTTING
SOBRIQUET	CONDESCENSION	SPARSE	DIABOLICAL	COHERENT

Caged Bird Vocabulary

INFUSE	TEDIOUS	CYNIC	APERTURES	PANDEMONIUM
EXPEDITIOUS	PROVINCIALS	CAPRICIOUSNESS	MOROSE	IMPERTINENCE
BLASPHEMOUS	EXCRUCIATING	FREE SPACE	CACOPHONY	GAUCHE
JAUNTINESS	ANACHRONISM	PALPABLE	LACERATION	ONEROUS
ELOCUTION	TRIBULATION	MASOCHISTS	FRIVOLOUS	RANCOR

Caged Bird Vocabulary

DESICCATED	EMBEZZLE	FRIVOLOUS	APPELLATIONS	PRETENSE
MARAUDING	DEFERENTIAL	EXPEDITIOUS	ANACHRONISM	IMPERTINENCE
MOLLIFIED	TRAMMELED	FREE SPACE	CYNIC	EXCRUCIATING
RANCOR	APPROBATION	BLASPHEMOUS	ABET	PALPABLE
RETRIBUTIVE	PROVINCIALS	INFUSE	SOBRIQUET	BOURGEOISIE

Caged Bird Vocabulary

ENIGMA	LACERATION	ELOCUTION	QUANDARY	MALAISE
CAPRICIOUSNESS	CAJOLED	PARANOIA	TROUBADOURS	DEFTNESS
REBUTTING	FLAMBOYANT	FREE SPACE	IMPASSIVITY	MOTE
SPARSE	DISSIPATE	TEDIOUS	DROLL	ONEROUS
OSTRACIZE	PERPETRATED	CONDESCENSION	OSTENSIBLY	INSCRUTABLE

Caged Bird Vocabulary

DEFTNESS	ENIGMA	APHORISMS	TRAMMELED	SOLICITOUS
COMMENSURATE	SUPERCILIOUS	MOROSE	RETRIBUTIVE	CONDESCENSION
OMINOUS	TRIBULATION	FREE SPACE	EXCRUCIATING	RANCOR
SPARSE	PLOY	LACERATION	MALAISE	TAFFETA
PROXIMITY	PRETENSE	APPELLATIONS	NONCHALANT	EMBEZZLE

Caged Bird Vocabulary

EXPEDITIOUS	COHERENT	ANACHRONISM	MOTE	ECUMENICAL
PROVINCIALS	PARANOIA	ABET	ELOCUTION	DROLL
SOBRIQUET	INFUSE	FREE SPACE	PERPETRATED	MOLLIFIED
INSCRUTABLE	DEXTEROUS	FRIVOLOUS	PALPABLE	CAJOLED
IMPERTINENCE	DISSIPATE	FLAMBOYANT	IMPASSIVITY	BLASPHEMOUS

Caged Bird Vocabulary

CYNIC	LACERATION	PARANOIA	FLORID	JAUNTINESS
SOBRIQUET	MALAISE	SPARSE	BOURGEOISIE	ADMONISHED
APHORISMS	TEDIOUS	FREE SPACE	TRIBULATION	EMBEZZLE
REBUTTING	RANCOR	OMINOUS	ESTHETIC	ENIGMA
PRETENSE	ANACHRONISM	ELOCUTION	PERPETRATED	TAFFETA

Caged Bird Vocabulary

DEXTEROUS	INSCRUTABLE	RETRIBUTIVE	PANDEMONIUM	DESICCATED
EXPEDITIOUS	MASOCHISTS	DEFTNESS	FRIVOLOUS	INFUSE
APPELLATIONS	ECUMENICAL	FREE SPACE	DEBUTANTE	IMPERTINENCE
PALPABLE	DIABOLICAL	MOTE	MARAUDING	EXCRUCIATING
SUPERCILIOUS	TROUBADOURS	CACOPHONY	PLOY	NONCHALANT

Caged Bird Vocabulary

DEXTEROUS	ADMONISHED	PLOY	APPELLATIONS	DROLL
CYNIC	OSTENSIBLY	CAJOLED	MALAISE	TAFFETA
DEFTNESS	IMPASSIVITY	FREE SPACE	TRAMMELED	CONDESCENSION
REBUTTING	EXPEDITIOUS	DISSIPATE	MOLLIFIED	NONCHALANT
SOBRIQUET	INFUSE	ECUMENICAL	BOURGEOISIE	APERTURES

Caged Bird Vocabulary

OSTRACIZE	PROVINCIALS	MASOCHISTS	ANACHRONISM	LACERATION
APPROBATION	TRIBULATION	RANCOR	PROXIMITY	ESTHETIC
CAPRICIOUSNESS	ABET	FREE SPACE	RETRIBUTIVE	GAUCHE
FLORID	COMMENSURATE	SOLICITOUS	TROUBADOURS	ELOCUTION
IMPERTINENCE	PERPETRATED	EXCRUCIATING	PRETENSE	FLAMBOYANT

Caged Bird Vocabulary

ADMONISHED	MOROSE	ENIGMA	CAPRICIOUSNESS	RETRIBUTIVE
ONEROUS	PANDEMONIUM	RANCOR	EXCRUCIATING	JAUNTINESS
DISSIPATE	ABET	FREE SPACE	EMBEZZLE	ANACHRONISM
INFUSE	ELOCUTION	INSCRUTABLE	SPARSE	TEDIOUS
DEBUTANTE	PLOY	DESICCATED	FLAMBOYANT	PROVINCIALS

Caged Bird Vocabulary

CYNIC	IMPERTINENCE	TRAMMELED	ECUMENICAL	PRETENSE
REBUTTING	APPROBATION	MOTE	TROUBADOURS	CONDESCENSION
MALAISE	PARANOIA	FREE SPACE	SOLICITOUS	MOLLIFIED
PROXIMITY	FLORID	BOURGEOISIE	LACERATION	SUPERCILIOUS
RAUCOUS	QUANDARY	BLASPHEMOUS	OMINOUS	MASOCHISTS

Caged Bird Vocabulary

DROLL	REBUTTING	CACOPHONY	ENIGMA	CAPRICIOUSNESS
OMINOUS	DEXTEROUS	MOLLIFIED	INSCRUTABLE	SOBRIQUET
IMPASSIVITY	CAJOLED	FREE SPACE	FRIVOLOUS	ONEROUS
MASOCHISTS	DEBUTANTE	COMMENSURATE	SUPERCILIOUS	ADMONISHED
ABET	DEFERENTIAL	LACERATION	PROVINCIALS	PALPABLE

Caged Bird Vocabulary

FLORID	FLAMBOYANT	QUANDARY	CYNIC	APHORISMS
OSTENSIBLY	MOTE	DESICCATED	ESTHETIC	TRIBULATION
INFUSE	TROUBADOURS	FREE SPACE	TAFFETA	DISSIPATE
BLASPHEMOUS	OSTRACIZE	ANACHRONISM	EXCRUCIATING	PRETENSE
APPROBATION	GAUCHE	DIABOLICAL	NONCHALANT	EXPEDITIOUS

Caged Bird Vocabulary

EXPEDITIOUS	SOLICITOUS	INFUSE	MOTE	SPARSE
DIABOLICAL	SUPERCILIOUS	INSCRUTABLE	TRAMMELED	RAUCOUS
CAPRICIOUSNESS	PRETENSE	FREE SPACE	ESTHETIC	ELOCUTION
CACOPHONY	COHERENT	ONEROUS	PROVINCIALS	MALAISE
ANACHRONISM	CONDESCENSION	IMPERTINENCE	FLORID	OSTRACIZE

Caged Bird Vocabulary

PARANOIA	PLOY	REBUTTING	ABET	APHORISMS
DEFERENTIAL	DEFTNESS	APPROBATION	NONCHALANT	RANCOR
MOROSE	RETRIBUTIVE	FREE SPACE	EXCRUCIATING	LACERATION
FLAMBOYANT	OMINOUS	MARAUDING	SOBRIQUET	PALPABLE
TRIBULATION	ADMONISHED	IMPASSIVITY	DESICCATED	MASOCHISTS

Caged Bird Vocabulary

PROXIMITY	DISSIPATE	PERPETRATED	EMBEZZLE	FRIVOLOUS
PANDEMONIUM	DROLL	LACERATION	ECUMENICAL	APHORISMS
DIABOLICAL	PROVINCIALS	FREE SPACE	SPARSE	RAUCOUS
GAUCHE	CACOPHONY	ELOCUTION	EXPEDITIOUS	CAPRICIOUSNESS
MASOCHISTS	MALAISE	SUPERCILIOUS	COMMENSURATE	IMPASSIVITY

Caged Bird Vocabulary

DEXTEROUS	APPELLATIONS	PARANOIA	MARAUDING	BLASPHEMOUS
DEFTNESS	ESTHETIC	BOURGEOISIE	COHERENT	ABET
TEDIOUS	DESICCATED	FREE SPACE	MOLLIFIED	RETRIBUTIVE
OSTENSIBLY	IMPERTINENCE	EXCRUCIATING	DEFERENTIAL	PALPABLE
INFUSE	CYNIC	QUANDARY	ANACHRONISM	RANCOR

Caged Bird Vocabulary

ABET	TRIBULATION	QUANDARY	PLOY	ELOCUTION
PARANOIA	MALAISE	MASOCHISTS	CONDESCENSION	CACOPHONY
APERTURES	ESTHETIC	FREE SPACE	RETRIBUTIVE	APPROBATION
PANDEMONIUM	REBUTTING	SOBRIQUET	CAPRICIOUSNESS	LACERATION
COMMENSURATE	CYNIC	DESICCATED	DEFTNESS	TEDIOUS

Caged Bird Vocabulary

RANCOR	DEXTEROUS	PROXIMITY	TROUBADOURS	BOURGEOISIE
OSTENSIBLY	COHERENT	EXCRUCIATING	PALPABLE	FLAMBOYANT
SUPERCILIOUS	DEFERENTIAL	FREE SPACE	FRIVOLOUS	IMPERTINENCE
ADMONISHED	PRETENSE	ONEROUS	OSTRACIZE	FLORID
DISSIPATE	SOLICITOUS	DROLL	PROVINCIALS	OMINOUS

Caged Bird Vocabulary

ADMONISHED	EMBEZZLE	MOLLIFIED	MALAISE	FRIVOLOUS
MOROSE	DIABOLICAL	JAUNTINESS	PROXIMITY	ABET
CAPRICIOUSNESS	MOTE	FREE SPACE	DEFTNESS	DEFERENTIAL
CYNIC	ONEROUS	DEXTEROUS	INSCRUTABLE	BOURGEOISIE
REBUTTING	OSTENSIBLY	RETRIBUTIVE	IMPASSIVITY	APPELLATIONS

Caged Bird Vocabulary

SPARSE	BLASPHEMOUS	CACOPHONY	TRIBULATION	ELOCUTION
GAUCHE	QUANDARY	PERPETRATED	SUPERCILIOUS	IMPERTINENCE
TROUBADOURS	MARAUDING	FREE SPACE	TEDIOUS	DESICCATED
FLAMBOYANT	ANACHRONISM	PALPABLE	OMINOUS	LACERATION
COMMENSURATE	DISSIPATE	APHORISMS	ECUMENICAL	MASOCHISTS

Caged Bird Vocabulary

CONDESCENSION	TEDIOUS	ADMONISHED	PANDEMONIUM	OSTRACIZE
APHORISMS	ESTHETIC	SOLICITOUS	EXCRUCIATING	MALAISE
PALPABLE	SPARSE	FREE SPACE	LACERATION	DEXTEROUS
ECUMENICAL	REBUTTING	DISSIPATE	CYNIC	DEBUTANTE
INSCRUTABLE	MARAUDING	QUANDARY	APERTURES	OSTENSIBLY

Caged Bird Vocabulary

JAUNTINESS	FLORID	EMBEZZLE	IMPASSIVITY	BLASPHEMOUS
MASOCHISTS	GAUCHE	TAFFETA	DESICCATED	TRAMMELED
RECRIMINATIONS	PROXIMITY	FREE SPACE	EXPEDITIOUS	PRETENSE
TRIBULATION	MOROSE	FLAMBOYANT	CAJOLED	ENIGMA
APPROBATION	FRIVOLOUS	MOLLIFIED	PROVINCIALS	CAPRICIOUSNESS

Caged Bird Vocabulary

MARAUDING	OSTENSIBLY	ENIGMA	ONEROUS	FLORID
TEDIOUS	DESICCATED	MOTE	REBUTTING	EMBEZZLE
TROUBADOURS	DEBUTANTE	FREE SPACE	DROLL	PARANOIA
NONCHALANT	CAPRICIOUSNESS	LACERATION	IMPERTINENCE	PERPETRATED
RETRIBUTIVE	CAJOLED	DIABOLICAL	ADMONISHED	EXPEDITIOUS

Caged Bird Vocabulary

INFUSE	DISSIPATE	GAUCHE	SUPERCILIOUS	DEFERENTIAL
CYNIC	SPARSE	BLASPHEMOUS	ANACHRONISM	COMMENSURATE
QUANDARY	SOLICITOUS	FREE SPACE	MASOCHISTS	FLAMBOYANT
PRETENSE	OMINOUS	TRAMMELED	DEFTNESS	PROVINCIALS
DEXTEROUS	MALAISE	COHERENT	OSTRACIZE	ESTHETIC

Caged Bird Vocabulary

LACERATION	IMPASSIVITY	MASOCHISTS	SOLICITOUS	RAUCOUS
DEXTEROUS	NONCHALANT	MARAUDING	EXPEDITIOUS	PROVINCIALS
ESTHETIC	INFUSE	FREE SPACE	PARANOIA	CYNIC
SUPERCILIOUS	MOTE	EMBEZZLE	FLORID	JAUNTINESS
APHORISMS	RETRIBUTIVE	TRAMMELED	PERPETRATED	ANACHRONISM

Caged Bird Vocabulary

FLAMBOYANT	DIABOLICAL	CONDESCENSION	SOBRIQUET	SPARSE
MALAISE	PROXIMITY	CAPRICIOUSNESS	GAUCHE	EXCRUCIATING
OMINOUS	TAFFETA	FREE SPACE	OSTENSIBLY	APPROBATION
BOURGEOISIE	ENIGMA	REBUTTING	PALPABLE	APPELLATIONS
PLOY	CACOPHONY	TEDIOUS	INSCRUTABLE	BLASPHEMOUS

www.ingramcontent.com/pod-product-compliance
Lightning Source LLC
Chambersburg PA
CBHW081453070526
44586CB00019B/2339